From Babylon to Bethlehem

From Babylon to Bethlehem

The People of God Between the Testaments

H.L. ELLISON

BAKER BOOK HOUSE
Grand Rapids, Michigan 49506

CONTENTS

ABBREVIATIONS

The normal literary abbreviations and those for the names of Biblical and Apocryphal books have been used. The following call for special mention.

Ant.	Josephus, *Antiquities of the Jews*
AV	Authorised, or King James Version of the Bible, 1611
Contra Ap.	Josephus, *Against Apion*
DOTT	D. Winton Thomas, *Documents from Old Testament Times*
JB	The Jerusalem Bible, 1966
LXX	The Septuagint—translation of OT into Greek before Christian era
Moffatt	J. Moffatt translation of the Bible, 1913, 1924, revised 1935
NEB	New English Bible, 1961, 1970
NT	New Testament
OT	Old Testament
RSV	Revised Standard Version, 1946, 1952
RV	Revised Version, 1881, 1884
Vita	Josephus, *Life*
War	Josephus, *The Jewish War*

Note:
The Genealogical Tables on pp. 127–130 incl. are taken, by kind permission of the author, from *Israel and the Nations* by F. F. Bruce.

PREFACE

By a strange quirk of history until recently the average Christian has tended to know more about the period between the Babylonian exile and the time of Jesus than has the average Jew. Because of the presence of the Books of the Maccabees in the Apocrypha some of their leading characters were regarded as pre-Christian heroes and martyrs along with the mighty men of the Old Testament. The works of Josephus, especially after Whiston's translation in Authorised Version style (1736), became recognized Sunday reading in stricter Christian homes. Both these sources remained unknown to the average Jew, until the rise of Zionism brought the story of the Maccabees back into favour.

Knowledge has seldom, however, meant understanding, even of the Biblical sources involved. This was partly due to the anti-Judaism which so quickly reared its ugly head in the Church. This was intensified last century by Wellhausen's views on post-exilic Judaism derived from his Hegelian presuppositions; this prevented several generations of scholars from doing justice to the ever increasing volume of information on the period.

This book seeks to serve a double purpose. On the one hand it tries to make the post-exilic books of the Bible more comprehensible so far as this can be done without a detailed exegesis. On the other it seeks to discover the main reasons why Palestinian Jewry rejected Jesus at least in the person of its leaders and why it went down to ruin less than forty years later. It is not one more history of the period, for there are enough of them, nor is it a description of the Judaism that lies behind the New Testament and modern Jewish Orthodoxy alike. Here again sufficient work has been done by others.

Most of the material has appeared in *The Hebrew Christian*, the quarterly journal of the International Hebrew Christian Alliance. In its present form the work is intended as a tribute to the organization for its Jubilee.

Since the book is intended for non-technical readers, Jehovah is used in preference to Yahweh and the traditional form of reference will be found for Josephus, for most readers will find Whiston's translation most readily available. Though the name Palestine was not applied to the whole country until after Bar Kochba's revolt, it has been used for the sake of simplicity.

Since there has been no desire to provide a detailed picture of the New Testament background, the last chapter could have been omitted. It was felt, however, that a brief outline of the last tragic years of the Jewish commonwealth was in place. Owing to the way in which the work came into being a certain amount of repetition was unavoidable, but it is hoped that it will not be found disturbing.

vii

Those wishing a more directly historical presentation of the subject will find it in, among others, E. Bevan, *Jerusalem under the High Priests* and F. F. Bruce, *Israel and the Nations*. The most thorough treatment is in Vol. II of Oesterley and Robinson, *A History of Israel*. For those wishing details of the Qumran discoveries F. F. Bruce, *Second Thoughts on the Dead Sea Scrolls* is probably the most suitable work.

Dawlish, Devon   H. L. Ellison
Lent 1975

1

THE IMPORTANCE OF THE
INTER-TESTAMENTAL PERIOD

We have probably all heard the gibe against much traditional Old Testament exegesis, "It takes all the blessings for the Church and leaves all the curses for the Jews." Proof for this attitude is found most readily in the chapter and page headings of Isa. 40–66 in older editions of the AV. That this attitude used to exist almost universally and is still to be widely found needs no proof. After all, it was the logical outcome of the assumption that the Church is Israel.

Our recognition that many past and present theologians and expositors have been wrong, does not justify our looking on them as fools. They were motivated by more than a blind, logical working out of their assumptions. When we compare the glowing descriptions in Isa. 40–55 with the humble reality in Ezra and Nehemiah, it is natural to ask ourselves whether there is really any link between them. Isa. 43:16–21 compares the return from Babylonia with the Exodus from Egypt and suggests that it will be even greater and more glorious.

From Babylonia there returned about 50,000 together with 7,537 slaves (Ezr. 2:64, 65). The total given in Ezr. 2:2–60 is 29,818, in Neh. 7:6–62 31,089, but both agree in a grand total of 42,360 (Ezr. 2:64, Neh. 7:66); the difference is to be explained by the larger figure including the women. The parallel passage in 1 Esdras 5:41 says, probably correctly, that these were those over twelve years of age. If we allow for the children as well, we reach the round figure suggested above.

A four month journey (cf. Ezr. 7:9) for such a large party was a very difficult undertaking, and it may very well be, as suggested by the internal structure of the list of those who returned, that they came in a number of groups. It was in any case a pitifully small number to restart the history of Israel, and there is no suggestion that they encountered any signal signs of God's favour to encourage them. They returned to a Judea that stretched from Bethel to about Beth-zur, north of Hebron, and from Jericho to the fringe of the coastal plain. Not a vestige of political independence was granted them, and until the time of Nehemiah they apparently formed part of the area under the Persian governor in Samaria, himself subject to the governor or satrap of the province "Beyond the River (Ezr. 5:63)." Their change of status has often been expressed by saying that they went into exile a nation and returned a church.

The purpose of this book is to show, as least in part, why there is such an apparent disparity between Isa. 40–55 and the events of the return and their sequel. It should not be forgotten that even in Isa. 40–48 there are darker passages, e.g. 48:1–5, 17–19, while the promises of 49–55 clearly depend on the work of the Servant. By the end of the book it may be clearer to the reader why the Servant was recognized by so few when he came, and why, therefore the to us mysterious Inter-Testamental period is of the utmost importance in the working out of God's purposes.

The period covered by this book begins in 538 B.C. and runs on to the death of Herod the Great in 4 B.C.; this is a considerably longer stretch of time than from the death of Queen Elizabeth I to our own days. During it the prophetic revelation of God ceased, there being only vestiges of it from the time of Malachi to the rise of John the Baptist, and we are almost devoid of accurate knowledge of the history of Judea until about 175 B.C. Even then our knowledge is superficial and partial, as was shown by the excitement caused by the discovery of Qumran and its manuscripts.

One of man's special abilities is to reach into the distant past and picture its events as though they were virtually present. He pays for this by often overlooking the length of time that has elapsed. So we miss the implications of Christ's genealogy in Matt. 1:1–17, viz. that from Abraham to David, from David to the exile, and from the exile to our Lord are comparable periods of time.

While this book must deal with history, for God's purposes and revelation are worked out in history, its real interest is in the development of Judaism during this period and in those factors which prepared the way for the coming of the Messiah. That is why it does not go down in detail to the destruction of Jerusalem and the Temple in A.D. 70. Those desiring a more purely historical treatment will find it, *inter alia*, in F. F. Bruce, *Israel and the Nations*.

2
THE SPIRITUAL EFFECTS OF THE BABYLONIAN EXILE

The three periods into which Matthew divided the genealogy of Jesus the Messiah are not merely three convenient subdivisions. From Abraham to David may fairly be called the period of promise. It is clear from Nathan's words to David in 2 Sam. 7 : 10, 11 that God did not consider that His promises of giving the land to Israel had been completely fulfilled till the time of David. Whatever we may think of the Israelite monarchy as an institution, the confirming of the Davidic dynasty was also a confirming of Israel's possession of the land. Throughout the period of the Judges right down to and including Saul we gain the impression that Israel, apart from Divine favour, could have been dispossessed by its neighbours, even though in many cases they were less numerous. Under David, however, Israel could even indulge in the luxury of a civil war without a single one of its neighbours taking advantage of the fact. Indeed Shobi, the brother of Hanun, king of Ammon, whom David had conquered and presumably killed, came to David's aid at the moment it was most needed (2 Sam. 17 : 27).

The second period is that of Israel's failure in spite of the fulfilment of God's promises. It is a pity we seldom take the time to read the books of Kings through at a sitting. It would give us a much more realistic picture of the way we pass from the dazzling emptiness of Solomon's glory through the growing weakness caused by civil war until we reach the inevitable grave of the exile. Both kingdoms shared a moment of revived power and glory, the North under Jeroboam II, the South a hundred and fifty years later under Josiah, and with both we discover that the glory was merely the iridescence of the soap bubble.

We are apt to think of the exiles as periods of punishment; once they were finished, return to the old was possible. Indeed the whole British-Israel concept is based on such a return being inevitable. Yet Jeremiah makes it clear that whatever God's mercy might yet do, exile marked a real change in relationship. Speaking of and probably to the ten-tribe Israel of Judah's unwillingness to learn the lesson, he says, "She (Judah) saw that for all the adulteries of that faithless one, Israel, I had sent her away with a decree of divorce" (Jer. 3 : 8).

The Bible is permeated with the concept of completeness. King and people, husband and wife, father and son, mother and daughter, master and servant; none of these pairings are meaningful, if one half or the other is lacking.

It is doubtful whether Biblical Israel ever thought that God's choice of them was influenced by any merit on their part. They had been chosen and made a people in election love and covenant faithfulness. But with only few exceptions they were convinced that God had chosen them because He needed them. As King He needed Israel as His people, as Husband He needed her as wife, as Father He needed him as son, as Master He needed him as servant. Israel would never have existed but for Jehovah,* but Jehovah was incomprehensible without Israel, at least to the popular mind.

Exile meant that Israel was no longer able to claim to be in covenant relationship with its God and had lost all the privileges that sprang from it, cf. Exod. 19:5, 6. It would be more accurate to say that, if it continued to enjoy any of them, it was out of pure grace; they could not be claimed as a right. Ezekiel was clear that when Nebuchadnezzar took Jehoiachin and his fellow-deportees to Babylonia it was an act of God's grace to save them from destruction, but he also stressed that it was a modified act of judgment in which "I have scattered them . . . and have become to them a sanctuary in small measure" (Ezek. 11:16).

The separation from the Temple and its subsequent destruction will have influenced those in Babylonia in two ways. For those who had not taken in the prophetic message, and they will have been the majority, the destruction of the Temple will have been the supreme, incredible sign of Jehovah's impotence. They believed that somehow He derived something from the sacrifices, something that He needed, the supreme gain He derived from having a people. In spite of Asaph's words, "Do I eat the flesh of bulls, or drink the blood of goats?" (Psa. 50:13), many will undoubtedly have thought that God did. Others will have thought that the smoke of the burnt offerings did carry up something real and necessary to Him. Therefore they will have believed that He had been defeated by the gods of the heathen.

For those who had learnt the prophetic lesson there remained another and possibly more agonizing problem. We have insufficient evidence to be able to say much about the individual's piety in his home during the time of the monarchy, how he prayed and worshipped, if indeed he did so privately. It is certain, however, that his public worship was inescapably tied up with sacrifice, whether it was at a local sanctuary or at the temple in Jerusalem. It did not matter whether it was his private sacrifice, or whether he merely associated himself with an offering brought for the community at large, the service centred round the sacrifices which had been brought. Already after Josiah's stringent centralization of sacrificial worship at Jerusalem there must have been searchings of heart among those who lived too far away from the capital to attend regularly. Now in exile all possibility of sacrificial worship had been removed.† Part of the sting in Psa. 137:3 is that "the Lord's song" had been part of the setting of the old sacrificial worship.

A living religion can never stand still for long; it is always adapting itself to

---

* Yahweh is indubitably nearer the original pronunciation of the sacred name, but I have preferred to retain the popular form Jehovah in the few cases where it is needed.

† A few scholars, basing themselves on Ezr. 8:17 and the example of the Elephantine temple (cf. p. 23), think there may have been some sacrifice in Babylonia; if so, it has left no mark in Scripture.

changing circumstances. But it can never really go back, however much it looks back. When a modern Christian denomination seeks to put the clock back and copy "the New Testament pattern," the new conformity is merely external; behind it lies an adaptation to new circumstances. Similarly the suggestion that the modern Israeli will rebuild the Temple and re-introduce the Mosaic system of sacrifices breaks down in the face of these facts. That Israel may build some form of building for worship in the *haram es-sherif*, the Temple area, cannot be ruled out as impossible, but the form of worship in it would be recognizable neither to Moses nor Caiaphas. In addition we should note that there is virtually no desire for it among Jewish religious leaders both inside and outside Israel.

In Babylonia the Jews could not go back to the religion of the Patriarchs and bring sacrifices wherever they might find themselves. A few may have done so, but there is no evidence that any such practice was wide-spread. The majority found themselves shut in to a religion without sacrifice but with no indication of a new direction to which to turn. Ezek. 40–48 shows that they could think only in terms of the restoration of the old. The heart-broken and almost hopeless mourning of Psa. 137 probably shows all that was left to most of them religiously. A similar hopelessness among those left in Judea may be found in Lamentations. For those that remained loyal to Jehovah, and most seem to have done so, nothing really remained but trust in the prophetic word of restoration and a looking forward to the renewing of the old.

Modern Old Testament scholarship has tended to look on the time of exile as one of great religious development. There is no evidence for this, and psychologically it is most improbable. The exiles will have been too stunned and too hopeless for that. Equally there is not the slightest evidence that the Synagogue, as it was later called, took its rise in Babylonia at this time, though it may well have done so later. The step from the sanctuary with its sacrifices to the synagogue with its study of the Mosaic law is far greater than we normally grasp.

I believe we shall do better to look on the exile in Babylonia in the same light as the sojourn in Egypt. It was far briefer, but it was long enough for the living links with the past to be broken, and so it provided the womb from which something essentially new could issue. Isaiah was fully justified in comparing the return to Palestine with the Exodus from Egypt, even though on the human level it might seem to be so much humbler.

The Palestine of the Return

The empire of Cyrus stretched from the frontiers of India to the Caucasus, the Aegean Sea, the Mediterranean and the frontier of Egypt. His son Cambyses conquered Egypt. For the first time redemption history* had moved into a wider geographical sphere than the Fertile Crescent.

Outlying provinces might revolt under the weaker of the Persian kings, seldom with much success, but, until the rise of Alexander the Great of Mace-

---

* This, or salvation history, is a technical term used by many for the history recorded in the Bible, for its purpose is solely to record those matters that have a bearing on the working out of God's redemption.

don, there was no one to challenge the might of Persia. This led to far-reaching results. The last vestiges of political autonomy vanished among the various peoples of the empire. The old city fortifications became a mere memory of past glory and lost all practical value, except perhaps that of holding up some marauding band until the imperial forces could arrive. On the other hand the imperial religion was no longer used as a weak means for keeping the subject peoples loyal. Rather they were encouraged and even commanded to worship their own gods, so that Persia might prosper by their aid.

The Persians left few records behind them, and so it is not likely that we shall ever know for certain when the teaching of Zoroaster (Zarathushtra) became the official religion of Persia. Darius I (521–485 B.C.) was certainly an adherent of it, and a passage like Isa. 45 : 5–7 gains its full meaning only if we assume that Cyrus was also.

Zoroastrianism is a complete and thorough-going dualism in which the great god of good and light with his angels stands opposed to the great god of evil and darkness with his angels. It was very easy and natural for the Persians to assume that the gods of loyal subject nations were among the great angelic helpers of Ahuramazda (Ormuzd), the god of good and light, while those of enemy tribes would be supporters of Ahriman, the spirit of evil. This explains the Persians' spirit of real religious tolerance within their empire. It enabled a Jewish religious community to be re-established with Jerusalem as its centre, and it provided that authoritarian backing without which Ezra's reforms might never have been carried through.

After Sargon, king of Assyria, had captured Samaria, he boasted in his inscriptions that he had built it up more gloriously than before. Things were very different in Judea after the destruction of Jerusalem by Nebuchadnezzar. W. F. Albright expresses it as follows.

> "A fair number of towns and fortresses of Judah have now been excavated in whole or in part; many other sites have been carefully examined to determine the approximate date of their last destruction. The results are uniform and conclusive: many towns were destroyed at the beginning of the sixth century B.C. and never again occupied; others were destroyed at that time and partly reoccupied at some later date; still others were destroyed and reoccupied after a long period of abandonment ... There is not a single known case where a town of Judah proper was continuously occupied through the exilic period" (*Archaeology of Palestine,* revised edit. pp. 141f.).

Whether Nebuchadnezzar intended to send new settlers to Judea after the Assyrian pattern must remain for ever hidden from us. It is clear, however, that he did not send them, and that he did not allow people from the neighbouring territories to come in and occupy the vacant towns and villages. So the land was kept open for the return by the hand of God. Some survivors of those left in the land there must have been (2 Ki. 25 : 12, Jer. 52 : 16), but they were obviously few and insignificant and they play no part in the story of renewal.

Even a fertile land will demand hard work if it has been neglected for almost half a century; how much greater must have been the difficulties in the hills of Judea. There were no economic reasons for the exiles to return, and it is not surprising that many were disheartened when they faced the stern realities.

Particularly annoying for them was that they had no direct access to the king, and that his will was not made known to them directly, but through the deputy governor in the administrative centre of Samaria. He could not directly block the emperor's will, but he could make it very difficult to carry out, and he could normally present the actions of the Jews in the worst possible light.

3

THE RETURN FROM EXILE

The story of the Exodus from Egypt is filled with miracles and signs, from the bush that burnt but was not consumed, up to the waters of the Sea of Reeds that flowed back, drowning the pursuing Egyptians. Compared with it the story of the return from Babylonia seems devoid of any manifestation of Divine action. Yet, when we look at the story more closely, God's mighty hand is seen at every turn. The spiritual baby needs the visibly wonderful at every turn; the mature believer should be able to see the working of God by faith, where the normal person can discern only the working out of natural law.

In the previous chapter it was mentioned that Nebuchadnezzar failed to send new settlers to Judea. Doubtless he was not aware that he was blindly obeying the promptings of God's Spirit. But God prepared for the return in another way also.

Josephus contains the "edifying" story (*Ant.* XI. i.2) that Cyrus somehow or other read the Book of Isaiah with its prophecy of Cyrus' rebuilding of the Temple. "Accordingly, when Cyrus read this, and admired the divine power, an earnest desire and ambition seized upon him to fulfil what was written". The Bible simply says, "The Lord stirred up the spirit of Cyrus king of Persia" (Ezr. 1:1). Obviously we have no right to dictate to the Holy Spirit what should be included in and what excluded from the salvation history of Israel. For all that it is hard to believe that if Josephus' account were true, it would not have been recorded in Ezra.

Archaeology suggests a simpler reason for Cyrus' action, but one that illustrates God's power to control the most complicated positions. Stress is laid in the Bible that on the three occasions Nebuchadnezzar forced Jerusalem's surrender he carried away some of the Temple vessels, cf. Dan. 1:1 f. for the first time, 2 Chr. 36:10 and Jer. 27:16 for the second and 2 Chr. 36:18 for the third. It seems clear enough that here was no question of mere looting, but that the vessels were intended to act as a substitute for the non-existent image of the imageless Jehovah. The insistence on the vessels in Jer. 27:16; 28:3 is adequate proof of this.

Their presence in Esagila, Marduk's temple in Babylon, was obviously to magnify the chief god of Babylon, who in the eyes of Nebuchadnezzar had given him the victory over Jehovah. Inscriptions make it clear that the Assyrian kings likewise removed the images of gods from conquered cities. Nebuchadnezzar had treated other conquered areas in the same way. We know from the Cyrus Cylinder, on which he commemorates his capture of Babylon, that in Esagila there were images of gods from a wide area up to and including the

Assyrian cities Nebuchadnezzar had conquered, destroying their sanctuaries. It may be that a break in the inscription hides the apparent failure to mention the western areas including Jerusalem. To these gods Cyrus then adds those of Sumer and Akkad (southern Mesopotamia or Babylonia proper) "whom to the anger of the lord of the gods", i.e. Marduk, Nabonidus had brought to Babylon.

We are not told exactly when or on what pretext Nabonidus, the father of Belshazzar and last king of Babylonia, had brought these gods and goddesses as visitors to Esagila. It may be that he thereby hoped to strengthen Babylon. In fact he so infuriated the priests of Marduk by this, and also apparently by changes in the ritual of Marduk, that they betrayed Babylon into Cyrus' hands. Evidently part of their compact was that these gods should be sent home, not merely Marduk's "guests" but also those he had conquered. This Cyrus did at once, and where the sanctuaries had been destroyed, those that had been deported were allowed to go home to rebuild the temples. Among them were the Jews.

For many such a reconstruction based on archaeological finds is much less attractive than the thought that God worked a manifest miracle for the Jews. A little thought should, however, convince us that it really magnifies our view of God, for it shows Him controlling the whole flow of events over a longer period, even Nabonidus' arrangement of an ecumenical get-together of the gods. In addition, however, it shows that Israel is no longer to be seen as the centre and purpose of His working except by the eye of faith. It had now been caught up in wider world events, but, for those who could see, these were so moulded that God's purposes were being worked out in Israel, even when Israel did not know it.

It was also an indirect announcement that the history of Israel was no longer to be lived out in a separated, specially guarded area, as Palestine had in some measure been until then, but that it was being swallowed up in world history. Consistently with this the background of the Bible, which from the time of Abraham had been confined to the "Fertile Crescent", including Egypt, was suddenly widened and was never again contracted to anything like the old limits.

The Cyrus Edicts

So far as the Jews were concerned Cyrus issued two edicts. One is found in Ezr. 6:3–5 in approximately its original Aramaic, the administrative language of the Persian Empire, at least from Babylonia westwards. It is clear that the text, as it has come down to us, is corrupt, for the temple's length is not mentioned; originally the dimensions will have been the same as those for Solomon's temple. Cyrus was willing to bear the chief cost of its rebuilding, but he was not giving the builders a blank cheque.

The other edict is now in Hebrew (Ezr. 1:2–4) and is doubtless a translation from the original Aramaic. There are no grounds for sharing the scepticism shown by so many about its authenticity. The Zoroastrian who, so long as he was in Babylon, could with a clear conscience attribute his mastery of the city to Marduk, could with an equally clear conscience attribute his lordship to Jehovah, the God of heaven, when dealing with Jews. The title "the God of heaven" is found already in Jonah 1 : 9, and it is in Ezra, Nehemiah and Daniel used regularly as a title for Jehovah. Almost certainly it had been coined by Israel, when it had to explain to polytheistic foreigners the unique functions of Jehovah. The language of v. 3 cannot come from a monotheist or even from one seriously devoted to the worship of Jehovah—"His people", "His god", "He is the God who is in Jerusalem" (RV, mg., RSV).

The edict, by using the phrase "all His people", covered all descendants of the Northern tribes who might have wished to return to Jerusalem, and so to Palestine, but there is no evidence that any did, except the descendants of those who had already moved to the South in the time of the monarchy. It is clear that the edict did not demand obedience but simply gave permission to those who wished to return. In the same way there was no compulsion on their neighbours to help them. It seems to have been a basic principle with these Persian kings that the welfare of the state—and, on the whole, Persian rule must normally have meant a real increase in prosperity—demanded the correct honouring of the gods of the subject peoples. So a contribution to the Jerusalem temple would have seemed something quite normal.

The Sheshbazzar to whom Cyrus entrusted the task of bringing back the vessels and of at least starting the rebuilding of the Temple was given the title *tirshata*, usually rendered governor (Ezr. 2 : 63) but meaning "he who is to be feared"; the modern English would be His Excellency. This title of respect was given to a *pechah*, who might be either a governor or a man charged with a special mission of importance like Sheshbazzar.

We cannot identify him with certainty. His name is Babylonian, but the title "prince of Judah" (Ezr. 1 : 8) and his deciding the standing of priests of doubtful genealogy (Ezr. 2 : 63) show that he was a Jew and apparently heir presumptive to the Davidic throne. There is therefore a wide-spread belief that he was the Shenazzar of 1 Chr. 3 : 18, probably the oldest surviving son of Jeconiah or Jehoiachin. The once popular view that it is only another name for Zerubbabel finds few supporters today. If either had been a Hebrew name, the supposition would have been taken more seriously.

The Roll of Honour

That the Chronicler was using old documents is shown by the interesting variation in language between Ezr. 1 : 11 and 2 : 1, i.e. "brought up . . . came up." The former chapter is clearly an official account, and so the returning exiles are said to be brought up by Sheshbazzar, the representative of the king of kings. But Ezr. 2 is the roll of honour of the founders of the renewed Israel, and so, because they acted at the call of God and not at the dictate of a heathen king, they are said to come up.

This roll of honour is found also in Neh. 7 : 6–73a and, as might have been expected, in 1 Esdras 5 : 7–46. Both Nehemiah and 1 Esdras indubitably correctly head the list with twelve names; we should insert Nahamani between Reelaiah and Mordecai in Ezr. 2 : 2—it need hardly be said that neither

Nehemiah nor Mordecai are the well known men of these names. The singling out of twelve leaders shows the conscious claim that those who returned claimed to be the renewed Israel, irrespective of what tribe they might belong to.

The second name on the list, Jeshua, is obviously the High Priest (Ezr. 3:2), who is called Joshua in Haggai and Zechariah. Presumably this had become the popular pronunciation in the post-exilic community. The high priests were relatively soon to become the *de facto* leaders of the Jews, and under the Hasmonean priest-kings the *de jure* rulers. Here the name of Zerubbabel stands significantly in first place.

It is unquestioned that the grandson of Jehoiachin is meant. In Ezr. 3:2, Hag. 1:1, Matt. 1:12, Lk. 3:27 he is the son of Shealtiel. But in 1 Chr. 3:19 he is the son of Pedaiah. The most likely explanation is that he was the physical son of Pedaiah, but reckoned as Shealtiel's through a levirate marriage. It is also unquestioned that he was the heir presumptive to the Davidic throne once Sheshbazzar, if he was indeed Shenazzar, who must have been an elderly man by this time, was out of the way. His place at the head of the list shows that there was a very strong political element in the return. The order in Ezr. 8:2 shows that it was not self-evident that the royal prince should be put in first place.

After the leaders we find the men of the people of Israel, in this context those who were not of the tribe of Levi (Ezr. 2:2b–35). The list contains an interesting duality. First we have the sons of named individuals, i.e. those who could trace their genealogy back to well-known figures of the past. In some cases the numbers completely exclude the possibility that they are the names of those led into exile. These run from vv. 3–20. Then come the men of certain places (vv. 21–28); a reference to the parallel passage in Nehemiah will show that throughout this section it should be "the men of . . ." We then return to the sons of named individuals (vv. 29–32), followed by the men of certain places (vv. 33, 34) and finally there are "the sons of Senaah" (v. 35). Some conclusions can be drawn from this variation.

Those who could trace their genealogies back to definitely known individuals and so through them to the basic structure of the tribes were the descendants of those who had been able to maintain their property and so their position in society during the increasing poverty of the later monarchy, i.e. "the people of the land" mentioned in 2 Ki. 11:13, 20; 21:24; 23:30, 35. Where only the home town is mentioned, we can be fairly sure that their ancestors had become landless and had lost their family links; it was the memory of a common home that had preserved their links with Israel during the exile. This explains why far fewer of this class returned. There was no longer traditional land to claim back in Judea, so the attractions of what they had been able to gain in Babylonia were the greater. No place names further south than Bethlehem and Netophah are mentioned, thus confirming the implication of Jer. 13:19, that Nebuchadnezzar had cut off the Negeb, the south of Judah, as a punishment, when he deposed Jehoiachin. There can be no doubt that the Edomite encroachment on southern Judea had already been carried through, though we do not find the name Idumea until later. This lasted until the time of John Hyrcanus (134–104 B.C.), who conquered Idumea and gave its inhabitants the choice of accepting Judaism or exile.

The peculiar structure of this list, with its alternation of groups, suggests strongly that we must presuppose at least two caravans with some space of time between them. With a total of about 50,000 this is highly probable. After all, the later return under Ezra numbered only some five thousand. Even under modern conditions the moving of 50,000 people over some 1,500 miles would be regarded as a major enterprise.

Then follow the Temple personnel. If we ignore the numerical variants in Nehemiah, we have for the people of Israel 24,144, but there are 4,289 priests, 341 Levites and 392 Temple slaves. If we include those of doubtful birth in Ezr. 2:59–62, somewhat over 652 in number, we discover that out of a total of nearly 30,000 over 5,000 were connected with the Temple, i.e. one in six; of these roughly four-fifths were priests.

We can deduce that there would almost certainly have been no return had there not been so many priests who longed once more to fulfil the task in society to which they had been called by God. On the other hand the low proportion of Levites shows how they had gradually been squeezed out of their proper place in worship and teaching by the priests. Many must have felt that return would mean semi-starvation. This is confirmed by the difficulty Ezra had in persuading Levites to join him (Ezr. 8:15). It is to be presumed that the Temple slaves and the descendants of Solomon's slaves returned because the exile had not meant the end of their servile status. Many of the exiles were theoretically Nebuchadnezzar's guests, and their slave property, so far as they could take it with them, remained their own. By origin these slaves were foreigners, but by this time they counted as Israelites, because they had adopted the religion of Israel, and in the course of the second temple's life they doubtless became regarded as Levites, for we have no evidence of their separate existence at a later date.

We have no further information about those who could not prove their descent (Ezr. 2:59, 60). They may well have been proselytes, cf. Isa. 56:6–8. Since their places of residence in exile cannot possibly have been the cause of their ignorance, we may rather imagine that special religious zeal ruling there caused them to face the long journey in spite of a possible rebuff at the end. Probably those who returned with Zerubbabel were far stricter than later generations, and we cannot doubt that their descendants were quickly absorbed into Israel. This is the more probable because a descendant of Hakkoz (Ezr. 2:61) is found as a priest in Ezr. 8:33, cf. Neh. 3:4, 21, although no priest able to consult Urim and Thummim had arisen (Ezr. 2:63). We know nothing of the fate of the sons of Barzillai.

It is fair to deduce then that those who returned were actuated by very differing motives and that socially they were very mixed. This helps to explain some of the strains and stresses we meet in the post-exilic prophets, as well as in Nehemiah.

4

THE REBUILDING OF THE TEMPLE

Safe arrival at Jerusalem by the returning exiles was immediately marked by the handing over of costly articles, money and priestly robes—had they been carefully treasured through the years of exile?—presumably to Joshua, the high priest, and his delegates (Ezr. 2:68f., Neh. 7:70ff.). It needs only a glance to show us that the text preserved in Nehemiah is superior, but the divergencies between them are not significant. It seems clear that the Chronicler abbreviated the text in Ezra. What is important is the statement in both books that "Some of the heads of fathers' houses gave to the work". This could be an underlining of the poverty of some of those who had returned, but it is more likely to have been a demonstrative refusal to contribute on the part of some. While it is again too hazardous to infer a reason for this attitude of mind, it is a clear warning of what was to come.

On the first religiously suitable day, the first day of Tishri (Ezr. 3:6), i.e. the Feast of Trumpets and the civil New Year, they recommenced the sacrifices, cf. Exod. 40:2, 1 Ki. 8:2. Here too an almost casual remark in the old story throws light on what was to be. We are told, "They set the altar in its place, for fear was upon them because of the peoples of the lands" (Ezr. 3:3). This can surely only mean that some of those that had returned—surely not the priests among them—had ceased under exilic conditions to see any spiritual purpose in sacrifices. They brought them now as a sort of bribery to ensure that God would protect them from their potential enemies. An element of textual difficulty hardly justifies us in changing the clause to its very opposite or deleting it altogether with Rudolph.*

There are many reasons why we cannot now envisage with any accuracy the exact task that faced the returned exiles in the rebuilding of the Temple. It is usual to contrast the approximately seven years needed by Solomon, with all the resources of his empire behind him (1 Ki. 6:37, 38), with the not quite four and half years needed by the rebuilders (Hag. 1:1, Ezr. 6:15), in spite of their poverty and limited resources, once they had started work in earnest.

The present temple area, the *haram es-sherif*, is beyond a doubt to be regarded as mainly the work of Herod the Great. Hence we do not know how much preliminary work on the site had to be done by Solomon. This would not have to be repeated by Zerubbabel and Joshua. We do not know either whether any effort was made to restore the elaborate system of storerooms round the walls of the sanctuary (1 Ki. 6:5, 6); probably not, though we must not forget that they figured in Herod's temple.

* *Esra und Nehemia* (1949).

There are, however, indications, especially Haggai's stress on timber (Hag. 1:4, 8), that the temple walls had not been razed to the ground. This would be the most likely interpretation of "When they came to the house of the Lord" (Ezr. 2:68), for the phrase seems to indicate at the very least an easily identified ruin. Probably the Temple had simply been set on fire (2 Ki. 25:9); the cedar panelling and roof would have burnt fiercely; the stone chambers round the walls would have collapsed as soon as the beams on which they were supported were burnt through; but the main building would have remained fairly intact. The special mention of cedars in Ezr. 3:7 has no bearing on the subject, because nothing less than timber of this type would provide the length to span the thirty foot width of the sanctuary and so support the roof. This view is not contradicted by the fact that the Chaldeans completely razed the walls and terraces that had come down from Jebusite times. The Temple was not the fortress it became latter in the Inter-Testamental period.

The various mentions of the laying of the foundations of the Temple in Ezra do not necessarily speak against this interpretation. In the Aramaic section of the book (4:8–6:18) RSV, NEB have, probably correctly, eliminated the mention in 6:3, while in 5:16 the meaning of the original may well be more vague. Certainly in the Hebrew section the traditional rendering is much too definite in 3:6, 10, 12, where the concept of foundation is derived from the verb *yasad* without any object added. But in 2 Chr. 24:27 the Chronicler uses *yasad* for repairs which, however far-reaching, certainly did not involve rebuilding the Temple from the foundations up. Probably a solemn ceremony implying a new beginning is intended. The sorrow of those who had seen Solomon's building (Ezr. 3:12) is best explained, if it was already plain how far short the new sanctuary would fall of the glories of the former house.

Though the Chronicler does not say so in as many words, he clearly implies in Ezr. 3:8 that the work of building and in particular that of laying the foundation was carried through by Zerubbabel and Joshua. In fact the studied anonymity of verse 10 seems to veil a minor comedy.

We took leave of Sheshbazzar in Ezr. 2:63, where "the governor" must surely refer to him. He passes without trace from the story only to reappear unexpectedly in Ezr. 5:14–16, where it is remembered that it was he who laid the foundation. Unless we accuse the elders of Jerusalem of deliberate lying, there seems to be only one way of explaining the apparent contradiction.

Sheshbazzar was Cyrus' commissioner to take back the Temple vessels (Ezr. 1:8, 11), and there can be little or no doubt that he was also entrusted with the responsibility of seeing that the Temple was rebuilt, or at least that the work was started on it. Hence he will have laid the foundation, even as the elders of Jerusalem claimed, but he will probably have returned to Cyrus shortly afterwards. The relative soundness of the old masonry will have justified him in so doing. His return would explain the presence of Cyrus' decree at Ecbatana (Ezr. 6:2) instead of its being treasured up in the Temple archives.

Sheshbazzar, even though he was "prince of Judah", was a Persian official acting for a heathen king—note that his name is not mentioned in Ezr. 2—so we are entitled to see Zerubbabel and Joshua taking over, when Sheshbazzar had discreetly withdrawn after laying the foundation, and repeating the ceremony. Only when a Persian satrap came nosing round (Ezr. 5:3) was it convenient and advisable to remember that it was Cyrus' representative who had begun the work.

The Samaritans

The returned exiles clearly expected trouble from their neighbours (Ezr. 3:3), but when it came, its form was obviously a surprise. The story begins by mentioning "the adversaries of Judah and Benjamin" (Ezr. 4:1), but as it develops, it becomes clear that only the Samaritans are intended. There is no evidence that others were at any time involved, for Tobiah the Ammonite and Geshem the Arab (Neh. 2:19) were almost certainly officials in the service of Sanballat, governor of Samaria.

When Samaria fell in 723 B.C. at the end of the reign of Shalmaneser V, the new king Sargon continued the policy introduced by Tiglath-pileser III and deported the cream of the population. His inscriptions indicate a figure between 27,270 and 27,290 for those taken away. To take their place leading citizens from other recently conquered areas were introduced (2 Ki. 17:24). They rapidly adopted a highly syncretistic worship, which helped towards assimilation with the Israelites who had been left in the land. With the growing tension between Assyria and Egypt, which was to result in the conquest of the latter, Esar-haddon (681–669 B.C.) introduced new colonists (Ezr. 4:2), and Ashur-bani-pal (669–c. 627 B.C.)—"the great and noble Osnappar" (Ezr. 4:10)—had to supplement their number once again. One reason, at least, for this will have been their rapid assimilation with the remnant of the indigenous population. This was so complete that somewhat later they claimed to be Ephraimites, as do their descendants to this day.

When 2 Kings 17 was written* the Samaritans still maintained their syncretistic worship (verse 34), but they must have abandoned it not so long after, perhaps as a result of Josiah's reforming activities (2 Chr. 34:6). Commonsense tells us that if they had still been semi-pagans, the Jewish leaders would have used this as their strongest argument against their helping in the rebuilding of the Jerusalem Temple.

There were doubtless two main motives behind the Samaritan leaders' request. On the one hand Josiah's thoroughgoing profanation of the traditional northern sanctuaries—Bethel (2 Ki. 23:15–20) is the example given in detail—had left Jerusalem the only site in the country with an unimpeachable history, for Nebuchadnezzar's destruction of the Temple had been purely secular, involving no profanation of the site—this is implicit in its continued use, at least in measure, as a place of worship (Jer. 41:4f.), and in the silence about any service of purification or resanctification, when the exiles returned. Then too, if they helped in the rebuilding, they would have a say in its administration, and through it in the internal affairs of Judah.

Modern writers like L. E. Browne* and Norman Snaith† have criticized the Judean leaders in bitter terms for their lack of love. They have seen in the delegation loyal Jehovah worshippers from the remnants of the northern tribes rather than half-assimilated foreigners. There is, however, little to be said for such a view, and there are only few who would support it today. This is not to deny that the old separation between North and South probably still rankled.

There is no evidence of any wish to exclude the Samaritans from the worship of the Jerusalem temple, and indeed their right to worship there seems always to have been conceded, provided, of course, that they accepted the Judean claims for Jerusalem. It may be questioned also whether it would have been politic to accept the offer. They had been given the task of rebuilding the Temple by Cyrus, and their very presence in Judea was based on this task. A report that they were not carrying through their task might have compromised their whole standing.

The Results of Opposition

Once Sheshbazzar had returned to Cyrus, Judea had no governor at its head appointed by the Persians. It was merely a subsection of Samaria, whose governor was a subordinate of the satrap of "Beyond the River". Though this is often denied, it seems to be convincingly proved by the language of Ezra 5 and 6. Throughout, Tattenai neither names nor knows any governor. Indeed Ezr. 5:3f. definitely precludes the possibility of there having been any officially appointed person who could have been automatically held responsible.

It is true that Ezr. 6:7 does explicitly mention the governor of the Jews—not of Judah, as normal usage would lead us to expect—but this is omitted by B, one of the main MSS of the Septuagint and also by the Syriac. In addition the Aramaic text, as it stands, is impossible. It is much easier, therefore, to regard "the governor of the Jews" as a later addition, which in 1 Esdras 6:27 has been expanded to "Zerubbabel, the servant of the Lord and governor of Judea", an impossible reading for an official letter. 1 Esdras also inserts "Zerubbabel" in 6:29, corresponding to Ezr. 6:9.

Appeal may be made to Hag. 1:1, 14; 2:21, where Zerubbabel is called "governor of Judah", though this title is not given in Zechariah. We need not for a moment doubt that the inhabitants of Judah regarded Zerubbabel as their head, for he was the heir presumptive of the Davidic throne; hence they will have given him the honorific title of governor. Indeed the Persians themselves may well have regarded him as the *de facto* head of the Jewish community. But that did not give him any independent status vis-a-vis the governor of Samaria. This freedom seems to have come first in the time and person of Nehemiah, which indeed explains the bitter hostility he had to face.

The Samaritan landed proprietors—"the people of the land" ('am ha-'aretz)—were able to intimidate the newcomers (Ezr. 4:4). In addition they were doubtless able to see to it that the grant from the royal treasury (Ezr. 6:4), which would have been taken from the funds of the satrapy, was with-

* L. E. Browne, *Early Judaism.*

† N. H. Snaith, *Studies in the Psalter.*

held. Their opposition was the more effective because much of Cyrus' attention was being given to wars in the east of his empire, while during the short reign of his successor Cambyses, the king's attention was absorbed by his conquest of Egypt.

We have already seen that there were disparate elements among those who returned, and that there were heads of fathers' houses who apparently had no interest in contributing to Temple funds. It is not surprising, therefore, that enthusiasm for the rebuilding rapidly evaporated, when the full costs fell on the corporate body of those who had returned.

There are many scholars who base themselves on Haggai, and to a less extent on Zechariah, and claim that this picture in Ezra is pure invention. They maintain that the failure to rebuild was purely due to lack of zeal and interest. They deny that any outside pressure was experienced, and they affirm that the work did not begin until the second year of Darius.

In practice we repeatedly find in the Old Testament differing evaluations of events when we read of them in the historical descriptions and then in the contemporary prophets. If we were to judge purely by the account in Kings, to say nothing of Chronicles, we should think that the reformations of Hezekiah and Josiah were outstanding successes. From Isaiah, Micah and Jeremiah we gain a very different picture, even if it comes mainly from their disdainful silence about the outward spring-cleaning.

The wise said quite truly:
"The sluggard says, 'There is a lion outside!
I shall be slain in the streets'" (Prov. 22 : 13).

The desires of the heart repeatedly find external justification why they should be carried out. Haggai was entirely correct, when he turned the searchlight of the Spirit on his contemporaries' motivations. But the Chronicler was equally correct, when he stressed the external influences that seemed to excuse the carrying out of the secret fears and motives of those who had returned. So the unfinished Temple remained as a mute rebuke to God's people for nineteen years.

5

THE WORK OF HAGGAI AND ZECHARIAH

One reason why the returned exiles were prepared to postpone the building of the Temple to an apparently more suitable time was undoubtedly their feeling that it was not strictly necessary. The ground was holy whether there was a building on it or not. Since the altar had been re-erected, sacrifices were being held as normal. It should not be forgotten that the ritual *inside* the sanctuary was a very small part of the total. There was no image of Jehovah to be placed in it, and the Ark had vanished; Jeremiah had commanded that it should not be remade (3:16). So the question was doubtless asked why there should be a temple building at all. Quite apart from the fact that they had been allowed to return from Babylonia for the express purpose of rebuilding it, their attitude was bound to be interpreted as lack of respect for their God by all who saw the ruins of the former temple.

It is hard to know how long this situation might have continued, had not the international situation suddenly exploded. Cyrus had died in battle in Central Asia in 529 B.C. and was succeeded by his son Cambyses. He promptly prepared for the invasion of Egypt, which his father had already planned. His victory was complete and in 525 he was crowned as Pharaoh. Instead of returning to Persia at once, his task completed, he tried to extend his conquests westward and southward. The loss of two armies coincided with the news of rebellion at home (522 B.C.).

According to the amiable way of ancient kings Cambyses had had his brother Smerdis secretly murdered before he invaded Egypt. Encouraged by the bad news coming from there the chief minister, the Patizeites, who had been left in charge in Persia, took advantage of the strong physical resemblance of his brother Gautama to the murdered Smerdis and placed him on the throne as son of Cyrus. Cambyses died on the way back from Egypt, and it did not take Darius, a cousin of the dead king, long to dispose of the usurper. But almost the whole of the Persian empire took the opportunity to revolt, and Darius needed three years of fighting to establish his claim to be king.

There is no evidence that the province Beyond-the-River, i.e. Syria, was caught up in the revolt, but everywhere there must have been widespread uncertainty as to what the future might hold. We may be certain that in Judea there were those who saw in Persia's difficulties the beginnings of the fulfilment of their own national hopes.

In the second year of Darius (520 B.C.), when the internal struggle in the Persian empire was at its height, two authentic prophetic voices were heard in Jerusalem; Haggai began his ministry in late August (Hag. 1:1) and Zechariah two months later (Zech. 1:1).

Superficially there is little to link Amos with Haggai. The former was a shepherd, a small-town dweller, living much of his life in the open. The latter probably lived in Jerusalem and was almost certainly a Levite—an argument like that of Hag. 2:11–14 comes from one familiar with the minutiae of the Temple ritual. But both were able in outstanding measure to apply spiritual logic to the events of the day. So much is this true of Haggai, that for most of his message he apparently rejects the title of prophet. Only in 2:20 do we find the regular phrase, "The word of the Lord came to Haggai"; elsewhere (1:1, 3; 2:1, 10) we have the exceptional expression "The word of the Lord came by Haggai", which could have been interpreted by his readers only as a virtual denial that he was a prophet.

He knew that the people had been sent back from Babylonia by God, and that He had done it for the express purpose that the Temple might be rebuilt. Hence they could not expect political freedom and prosperity until God had seen their willingness to carry out their primary task. His reading of their position was confirmed by their economic plight. From the first, cf. Deut, 11:11–17, it had been stressed that rainfall and agricultural prosperity would depend on God and the people's attitude towards Him. So the drought that had plagued the people (1:6–11) could have been caused only by their sins, and of these the most obvious was the failure to rebuild the Temple. It must be remembered that drought was always regarded as a manifest sign of God's anger.

The date of his first message, the beginning of the sixth month, is significant. The seventh month, Tishri, is the climax of the Jewish religious year. The Feast of Trumpets, the civil New Year (*rosh ha-shanah*), was followed by the Day of Atonement (*yom kippur*), though this had still to develop the outstanding importance it had in the time of Christ, and even more later; this in turn was followed by the Feast of Tabernacles. In addition, the ancient hope that this month would usher in the Day of the Lord had certainly not lost its vitality, cf. Hag. 2:6f., 21f. So the prophet's call to build was virtually a challenge. How could his hearers expect God to come to them, if He had no house to come to? He was giving them a month to respond.

We may infer from Ezr. 5:1 that Zechariah actively supported Haggai's efforts. In his recorded messages in chs. 1–8,* however, he seems to take for granted that the Temple would be completed and goes on from there.

God or Walls

When we look at Zech. 1–8 from the vantage ground of the New Testament and of nearly two thousand years of waiting for Christ's return, it is easy enough to see that they look to the future as well as to the prophet's own time, and indeed that some of his visions could not have found their fulfilment then. They range from the vision of Jerusalem as the centre of God's rule (1:7–17) to one of God's angelic armies patrolling the whole world (6:1–8). It is to be

---

* Quite apart from questions of authorship, chs. 9–14 throw very little light on the history and conditions of this time.

noted that in the first vision Zechariah made explicit what was implicit in Haggai's message. The angel of Jehovah is seen in the glen (the valley of Kedron?) outside the ruined city walls, obviously because the Temple itself was not ready for Him to enter.

The third vision (2:1–5) presented a message, the reaction to which was later to provide a turning point in Jewry's development. It was solemnly declared that Jerusalem no longer needed a city wall for safety. The ancient Near-East, as we know it in the Bible, was a land of fortified settlements, large and small. Archaeology has shown us that these city walls go back almost to the beginnings of identifiable civilization, cf. Gen. 4:17. The oldest wall of Jericho has been dated about 7000 B.C. In many cases "fortress" would give the sense better, and often the Old Testament "cities" were no more than walled villages. There were, of course, many villages and hamlets without any form of protection, but their inhabitants expected to be able to take refuge in the nearest fortified settlement in case of need. In the Old Testament such villages are called the daughters of the fortified towns on which they depended. This pattern remained unchanged right down to the fall of the Babylonian empire. The Assyrian and Babylonian kings knew that a fortified town was a potential centre of rebellion; they had to tolerate them, for they could not guarantee speedy protection for their vassals.

With the rise of Persia to world power the position changed radically. For the first time there existed a state without any enemy that could effectively challenge it. Once Cambyses had rounded out its frontiers by the capture of Egypt, the only question was how much further it could extend its lines of communication. It was this far more than Greek gallantry that checked Persia's westward march. Under these conditions city walls ceased to be a necessity and became mainly a matter of prestige. Where they existed they were allowed to remain, but the re-erecting of what had been destroyed or the building of new fortifications was regarded as denying the value of Persian protection and an indication that revolt was intended. Zechariah assured the Jews that they needed neither protection nor prestige, for both would be amply provided by God's presence. The moment for spiritual decision lay the best part of a century ahead, but the very fact of the prophecy shows that there were those in Jerusalem who yearned for the protection and prestige of the past.

Tattenai

Fortunately Haggai and Zechariah were able to persuade the people to concentrate on the building of the Temple. Whatever the Samaritans may have thought about it, they had neither the power nor authority to interfere, nor would there be ears at court willing to listen to charges against the Jews in a time of war and upheaval, cf. Ezr. 4:5. But as peace began to be established, Tattenai, the satrap of Beyond-the-River, began to hear rumous of illegal acts in Jerusalem and decided that he had better look into them. Probably a year or a little more had elapsed—"at the same time" (Ezr. 5:3) is a vague term—and he seems to have combined his investigation with his first official tour of inspection, for he apparently had his sub-governors with him (Ezr. 5:6; 6:6).

There is no suggestion that the governor of Samaria was able to play any special part; Shethar-bozenai was probably Tattenai's official secretary.

There is no sign of hostility in Tattenai's question (Ezr. 5 : 3); indeed its form suggested that he expected that there was some legal justification for what was happening. Three years of administrative chaos would make a satrap cautious of jumping to conclusions. Hence he saw no reason for interfering until Darius should confirm that such a decree existed and what his royal will might be (Ezr. 5 : 17).

This time the Samaritans, or whoever had lodged the complaint, had seriously overreached themselves. First of all the decree was found (Ezr. 6 : 3–5), and secondly it so agreed with Darius' Zoroastrian religious policy that he positively wished its implementation. Hence the Jews suddenly discovered that work begun in poverty now had the full financial backing of the Persian authorities, without any possibility of spiteful enemies whispering into the satrap's ears. Haggai had promised God's physical blessing on the people, if they would get to work. It is not likely that he foresaw that the bulk of the heavy expenditure would be carried by the authorities. There was, in addition, for the time being at least, even financial support for the Temple cultus. The Persian concept was that such worship and sacrifice rightly carried on would be for the benefit of the empire as a whole. So in 515 B.C. the building was finished. It might be humble compared with what had been, but it was to serve until Herod the Great gradually rebuilt it in the closing years of the first century B.C.

Zerubbabel

Both Haggai and Zechariah gave Zerubbabel great and precious promises. The former virtually assured him that he was God's Messiah (2 : 21ff.); if the term was not used, it was probably a precaution lest the oracle should be reported by spies to the Persian authorities. For the same reason the latter obscured his message by linking it with the high priest (3 : 8; 6 : 12f.). It would not have been misunderstood by his Jewish hearers, for steeped in the past as they were, they must have understood that only a descendant of David could be intended. The very much later idea—we meet it first late in the second century B.C.—that there might be a Messiah from "the house of Levi" was a product of the fact that the high priests had been for so long the heads of the Jewish community, until under the Hasmoneans they became for a short time priest-kings.

In one way the message found its justification in the fact that Zerubbabel was the leader of a new Israel, of a new beginning, just as when Jesus the true Messiah came He was to make a new covenant with His people. Then too Zerubbabel is one of the few names that appears in both the genealogies of our Lord (Matt. 1 : 12, 13; Luke 3 : 27). From him indeed the Messiah was to spring, and so all the other contemporary descendants of David were eliminated from the hope.

However we interpret the prophecies, something happened. From this time on the descendants of David, so to speak, go underground. They play no further part in the history of their people. We find that the leadership of the

Judean community is virtually entirely in the hands of the high priests. It is not unreasonable to think that Zerubbabel could not wait God's time. If that is so, what he did is shrouded in silence and we have no information about his fate. Only on the assumption of drastic action by the Persian authorities can we explain the later obscurity of David's descendants, even when Judea became independent. We have already noted that by the time of Ezra priestly exiles returning from Babylonia took precedence over the descendants of David (Ezr. 8 : 1f.). In 140 B.C., when he had at last made Judea independent, Simon the Hasmonean was recognized as civil head of the state as well as high priest without anyone apparently suggesting that such a position should be reserved for the heir of the house of David. It is true that the Pharisees broke with his son John Hyrcanus, because he adopted the royal title, but it was the title, not the authority, they objected to.

All this showed that Jewry had apparently acquiesced in becoming a religious community instead of an independent nation. For centuries there were few signs that a real national consciousness still lived on beneath the surface.

FROM ZERUBBABEL TO EZRA
AND NEHEMIAH

From the completion of the second temple in 516 B.C. to Malachi some time in the first half of the fifth century B.C. virtually complete darkness falls on the history of the Jews. There is merely a gleam of light from the so-called Elephantine Papyri.

The first cataract on the Nile at the modern Aswan (the Syene of Ezek. 29:10; 30:6) was the normal and natural southern frontier of Egypt. There in the Nile there is an island formerly called Yeb, but now Elephantine. About 587 B.C. Pharaoh Psammeticus settled a "Jewish" military colony on this island to guard the frontier against the Ethiopians to the south. It is normally assumed that they were Jews who had entered the land before the destruction of Jerusalem by Nebuchadnezzar, but Oesterley brings forward a strong argument that they were descendants of Israelite exiles in Mesopotamia who entered Egypt willingly or unwillingly, when Ashur-bani-pal conquered the land in 667 B.C.* If this is so, they may have called themselves Jews because of the large influx from Judea in Nebuchadnezzar's time, cf. Jer. 44:1, 15.

Be that as it may, finds of papyrus documents on the island, all written in Aramaic, show that they had built themselves a temple, where they worshipped Yahu, i.e. Yahweh or Jehovah. In addition Anath-yahu, Anath-bethel, Eshem-bethel and Cherem-bethel were worshipped. We cannot interpret these names with certainty. It is likely that Bethel, i.e. the House of God, is merely a reverential replacement for Yahu. It is almost certain that we have the ascription of a wife Anath to Yahu, something that formed part of Canaanized Israelite religion throughout its history, cf. Jer. 7:18; 44:17, 25. There may have been as well the worship of a son. There is no reason for thinking that their cultus, which caused much ill-will among their Egyptian neighbours because it involved the sacrifice of bulls, differed in any significant degree from the Mosaic one. It is not surprising that some at any rate in the community were prepared to swear by Egyptian gods in legal matters. Laxity rather than syncretism would lie behind it.

In spite of its irregularities the colony was clearly regarded as Jewish. One of the most interesting of the documents found is an order from the Persian king Darius II, dated in his fifth year, i.e. 410 B.C., concerning the keeping of the feast of Unleavened Bread. Much of it is missing, and it is almost universally assumed that the Passover must have been mentioned as well. For our purposes it is of no importance whether it reached Elephantine through the Persian authorities or the Jewish priestly leaders in Jerusalem. A Jewish official,

* Oesterley and Robinson, *A History of Israel*, Vol. II, pp. 159–165.

Hananiah, was certainly involved. What is important is that this community on the fringe of the Persian empire was known as Jewish and treated as such. The supervision exercised over their worship must have been the same wherever there were Jewish communities. The detailed nature of the instructions helps us to understand how the somewhat earlier activity of Ezra was possible.

We know from other papyri that the temple was destroyed in 410 B.C. by the Egyptians of the neighbourhood. This was probably during the absence of the Persian governor. An appeal to a Persian official whose name has been lost, was unsuccessful. The leaders then wrote to the high priest and his associates in Jerusalem. When this failed they wrote in 408 B.C. to Bagoas, the Persian governor in Jerusalem and sent a similar letter to the sons of Sanballat, governor of Samaria. These two letters produced a favourable reply from Bagoas and Delaiah the son of Sanballat, but it is not known whether the temple was ever rebuilt. It may well be that red tape held up matters until Persian power came to an end in Egypt in 404 B.C. All this shows that the inhabitants of Yeb thought themselves proper Jews and took for granted that the Jerusalem priests would rally to their support. It throws much light on the background of Malachi and even more on the greatness of the achievement of Ezra and Nehemiah.

Malachi

Malachi's date must be inferred, partly from his position in the Hebrew canon of the Prophets, partly from the content of his message. The mention of the destruction and devastation of Edom (1:3, 4) is no real help, for the date when the Nabatean Arabs drove the Edomites out of their traditional territory cannot be accurately fixed.

There is no doubt at all that he is earlier than Ezra and Nehemiah, though he may very possibly have lived to see their reforms. The general atmosphere of despondency is of a very different type to that found in Haggai. So we shall be fairly safe in placing him only shortly before the activity of Ezra and Nehemiah.

The first sign of despondency was that God's love was doubted (1:2). This points to hopes deeply disappointed. Haggai and Zechariah had stirred up Jewish expectations to a very high pitch. Presumably the conditions of drought pictured by the former (1:6) had passed—certainly Malachi does not mention them—but the agricultural position had remained poor (3:10, 11). Judea was in any case a poor land and off the main trade routes. It had to wait until Hasmonean times to possess the coastal plain through which the main trade route ran. In addition, with Phoenicia and Egypt firmly in Persian hands, most of the trade to and from Egypt was carried by ship instead of crossing the desert between Philistia and Egypt; thus Judea was left in a backwater.

Most painful of all, however, was the complete lack of political freedom. Whether Zerubbabel lost his influence and possibly his life through foolish preparations for rebellion or simply through the steady extension of the Persian policy which allowed full religious autonomy and denied any and every form of political self-determination we shall probably never know. The fact that by

Malachi's time the public representative of the Jews was now the high priest, cf. the appeal to him by the community at Elephantine, underlined the loss of all national as contrasted with religious standing. The return from exile had made the charge that God was powerless, unreal and impossible. So the only explanation the ordinary man could find was that God did not care.

It was this attitude that led to Malachi's second charge, that the priests were offering ritually inadequate and unacceptable animals in sacrifice (1:6–14)—note RSV, NEB "food" (v. 7). There is no suggestion that Malachi was thinking primarily of the priests' own sacrifices. Normally priests tend to be overcareful and particular without any thought or care for the position of the worshipper. But in Malachi's day they were obviously glad to get sacrifices at all. The people, thinking that God had lost interest in them, had lost interest in God. They were only concerned with what they could obtain from God, so they did not see why they should give Him of their best.

This willingness by the priests to accept the second best and ritually inadequate was only one phase of a greater evil. In their capacity as religious teachers the priests were prepared to water down the law (2:1–9). This was done not out of pity for the poor, as was sometimes the case later in the first century A.D. with the Hillelite Pharisees, but to keep the favour of the civil leaders. It had already led to their being despised (2:9). Here again the underlying concept seems to have been that a God who had lost interest in His people was not likely to be concerned with whether His laws were being strictly observed.

Though there is no evidence for a corruption of religion of the type seen at Elephantine, it was certainly knocking at the door. A wave of mixed marriages had begun (2:11). Unless there is a reference to an otherwise unknown marriage of a priest of high standing or of the head of the Davidic house, "the daughter of a foreign god" is a collective, referring to the foreign wives in general. In any case it implies that these women made no pretence of accepting the religion of their husbands; this must be remembered when we come to consider Ezra's and Nehemiah's reactions to the mixed marriages they found already in existence. To make matters worse, in order to be able to take foreign wives they had first divorced their Jewish ones (2:14). Since polygamy was still practised, it shows that the new wives had demanded that they be mistresses in their new homes. So clearly there were political or economic motivations behind these marriages. To divorce the old to please the new was a flagrant breach of Deut. 24:1–4. However we are to interpret "some indecency" (RSV), or "something shameful" (NEB), which the husband found in his wife, it was bound in most cases to have shown itself much earlier in their marriage. These highly placed men, for there is really no reason to think that many of the poorer were involved, for the sake of gain had deliberately thrown overboard the wives they had lived with for years and had married those who were bound to bring religious corruption into the people. Once again, if God did not care, why should they?

Things had gone so far that all benefit from religion was denied (2:17; 3:13–15). Not only had God lost interest in them nationally, but He was not even prepared to be the guardian of public morality. So the old evils of the monarchy, which had been repeatedly condemned by the prophets, were re-appearing (3:5).

Because Malachi is generally handled timelessly in the pulpit, with little or no reference to its background, it is seldom realized how serious the position in Judea had become. If God had not raised up Ezra and Nehemiah, all the lessons of the exile might have been quickly unlearnt.

The Tragedy of the Walls

Today there is unanimity among scholars of all shades of opinion that the passage Ezr. 4:6–23 is an interruption in the story of the rebuilding of the Temple, and that 4:24 is the immediate continuation of 4:5. 4:6 does not mention the Temple and 4:7–23 deals specifically with the walls of Jerusalem and not with the Temple. There is nothing surprising in this, for more frequently than is often realized Old Testament writers place material out of strict chronological order so as to prevent the interruption of the main narrative.

For reasons which are never hinted at, still less explained, the Jews began to rebuild the walls of Jerusalem, although Zechariah in his day had been able to dissuade them (Zech. 2:1–5). The suggestion made by Stafford Wright* that the impulse had come from the enthusiasm engendered by Ezra's reform of mixed marriages is one for which there is no vestige of evidence. We must always remember that the attractiveness of a theory is never a proof of its truth. Our historian sees no point in going into detail; his motive is to show the inveterate hatred of the enemies of the Jews and he lets us see it through their own eyes. Quite naturally Rehum, Shimshai and the rest had no interest in the true motives of the builders, even if they were known to them.

It was pointed out in the last chapter that under the Persians fortifications had become virtually unnecessary and were mainly a matter of prestige. In connection with the rebuilding of the Temple we saw that any major building scheme needed the consent of the central authorities; how much more the building or rebuilding of city walls. We need feel no surprise that Artaxerxes put the worst construction on the unauthorized move in Jerusalem.

Ezra tells of two complaints made by the enemies of the Jews during the reign of Artaxerxes I. The former (4:7) seems to have been of a general nature and apparently had no special result, except perhaps that it may have made the king suspicious. The latter (4:8–16) was much more serious. Rehum was probably governor of Samaria and Shimshai his official second-in-command. This gave weight to their accusations. For all that the royal reply shows that the king's advisers realized that local jealousies were playing a part. That which had been done illegally had to be stopped and, if need be, undone, but the possibility of future permission was held out.

How much time was granted the builders before the royal answer came we do not know, but it will hardly have been less than six months. Recent excavations by Miss Kenyon have shown how thorough had been the destruction caused by Nebuchadnezzar's troops. If Nehemiah was later to complete his work in fifty-two days (Neh. 6:15), it can only mean that much of his task was

* J. Stafford Wright, *The Date of Ezra's Coming to Jerusalem²* (1958).

repair rather than rebuilding from ground level. There could have been no question of repairing the shambles left by the Babylonians; in some places Nehemiah's wall even followed another line than that of the Jebusite and Davidic wall. So it is a reasonable conclusion that Nehemiah and Jerusalem owed more to this apparent failure than is generally recognized.

We are told that the Samaritans made them cease "by force and power" (4:23), i.e. by armed force. They pretended that the city had to be captured by force of arms, and in so doing they created as much damage as they could. But once it was captured, they had to desist, for the royal decree did not cover a pulling down of what had gone up. So Nehemiah found much done to help him, when the time came.

Had the inhabitants of Judea had sufficient trust in God to accept Zechariah's vision of an unfortified city, the history of the Jews and of Jerusalem would have been very different, but this was too much to expect of those to whom Malachi's message had come. We have to bear testimony, however, to them that having chosen the second best they played their part well.

7
NEHEMIAH

At the beginning of this century there were those who questioned whether Ezra had ever existed, but there were very few who found difficulty in the apparent Biblical order of Ezra before Nehemiah. Today few, if any, query Ezra's existence and work, but the question of the relationship of the two men to one another is wide open.

The superficial reader normally assumes that Ezra (Ezr. 7:7) came to Jerusalem some thirteen years before Nehemiah (Neh. 1:1; 2:1) and joined forces with him, when he arrived. When Nehemiah's priority in time was first suggested, it was opposed by liberals as strongly as by conservatives. A stage has now been reached where it is acknowledged that there is little evidence one way or the other. The main points stressed today may be found in the Additional Note at the end of the chapter.

A valuable outcome of the controversy has been that today we have a clearer idea of the work and importance of the two men. We now realize that, though they probably had a common religious outlook, their activity was essentially distinct in motivation and purpose. Hence it seems wiser to ignore the controversy and to deal with the two men seperately.

Our knowledge of Nehemiah comes entirely from the Biblical book bearing his name. In Hebrew MSS., not in the printed Bible, it forms part of Ezra. It is generally recognized that it is a sort of appendix to Ezra and that it has been extracted from Nehemiah's diary, or memoirs, to use the usual term. Under circumstances unknown to us, parts of Ezra were woven into these extracts. We can recognize them easily by their style and the absence of the first person singular. The most important sections are 7:73b–9:37; 11:3–36; 12:1–26. Josephus (*Ant.* XI. v. 6–8) clearly had no information apart from our present book, and this he partly misunderstood.

We know nothing of Nehemiah's family beyond his father's name, Hacaliah (1:1; 10:1), or how he came to be attached to the Persian court. He was one of the royal cup-bearers (1:11); quite apart from the fact that there must have been a number of such officials (note that three months elapsed between 1:1 and 2:1 without Nehemiah's being called on to perform his duties), this is the correct translation of the Hebrew. It follows that he was in fact a member of the Persian civil service as well, but it is impossible to suggest what his post may have been, for such household posts were normally linked with other duties. His later activities with their high efficiency suggest that it involved administrative work of some importance. It is not likely that Artaxerxes would have appointed him as governor unless he knew that he had some qualifications for

28

the post. His position at court and at least one phrase in his Memoirs (6:11) suggest that he was a eunuch, and this is expressly stated in the LXX, though this could be no more than an inference.

A man in his position would have known of Artaxerxes' order about the walls of Jerusalem (Ezr. 4:17–22), but evidently the report that came back merely stated that the king's instructions had been carried out. Gradually the official report will have been amplified by rumours, until in desperation he received permission for his brother, Hanani, to visit Jerusalem. In the winter of 446 B.C. he returned with some Jerusalemites (1:2). Since Nisan (2:1) was the first month of the royal year, we must obviously read "nineteenth" in 1:1; the error, which also includes the omission of the king's name, is due to haplography. The picture they gave far exceeded Nehemiah's worst fears.

The popular, superficial view, which Josephus shared (*Ant*. XI.v.6), is that the destruction described was that carried out by Nebuzaradan at Nebuchadnezzar's orders (2 Kings, 25:8–10). But this had been done in 586 B.C., well over a century earlier. Nehemiah will have learnt of it as a little boy, and many from Jerusalem will have come and gone in the interval. To hold such a view one would have to adopt Bullinger's hair-brained theory, put forward in the *Companion Bible*, that Artaxerxes was not the first Persian king of that name (464–423 B.C.), but a Median king acting as Nebuchadnezzar's regent during his seven years of madness (Dan. 4). He may well have first been turned to it by Josephus' belief that Nehemiah had been taken into captivity by Nebuchadnezzar, but as with so many of his ingenious explanations, he has found few to follow him.

Once we realize that Neh. 1:3 is referring to a later and quite recent act of destruction, we are able to date and evaluate Ezr. 4:7–23 as was done in the previous chapter. We also realize one of the contributory causes of Nehemiah's fear. He intended asking the king virtually to countermand his previous order. It is true that a loophole had been left (Ezr. 4:21), but the task Nehemiah was taking on himself involved him in no little danger.

The Building of the Walls

When the time came for Nehemiah to go on duty again, his mourning and fasting had left their marks on him; this was immediately noticed by the king's keen eye, as his cup-bearer brought him the royal cup. Since the highest honour that could be offered a subject of the king of Persia was to be allowed to enter the royal presence—note the hedging round of the royal person in Est. 4:11—it is clear that sadness was in itself an affront to his majesty, an affront that would normally be punished by death. The king's question made Nehemiah realize that it was a case of now or never.

His words may have been bold, but we cannot doubt that his knees knocked together. It should be noted that he very carefully did not mention the name of Jerusalem; it might have reminded the king too easily of his fairly recent decree. His explanation of his sadness was based primarily on filial piety, "the place of my fathers' sepulchres". The king's answer, "For what do you make request?", was equivalent to a recognition that Nehemiah's signs of grief were justified.

Nehemiah sent up a wordless prayer to "the God of heaven", apparently the official title of Jehovah among the Persians, cf. Ezr. 1:2; 5:11; 6:9, and asked for permission to rebuild. Even now he did not mention the name of Jerusalem, though the mention of Judah would have made its identification easy, had the king wished to take the trouble. At this point it is mentioned that the queen, the king's main wife, was sitting with him. This suggests on the one hand that it was a fairly informal occasion, for the queen would not normally appear at a larger dinner party, cf. Est. 1:10ff. That meant too that those courtiers who had been bribed by the Samaritans, cf. Ezr. 4:5, were not present to raise any objection. On the other hand it must mean that Nehemiah had somehow won the queen's favour. The suggestion sometimes made that she was Esther has nothing to commend it, for she belonged to the previous reign, that of Xerxes. It does, however, support the idea that Nehemiah was a eunuch with access to the harem.

Artaxerxes gave him leave of absence for a limited period of time (2:6). Nehemiah does not mention how long it was, because it was clearly lengthened at a later date. It could hardly have been the twelve years that elapsed before he returned to report (5:14). What is more, there is no suggestion that he was made governor at this point, though this was soon added. It is likely that the queen continued to pull strings on his behalf. Nehemiah kept his requests moderate, asking merely for a passport and an order for timber. The king gave him in addition an official escort.

As the story develops, it becomes clear that Nehemiah was a rich man. He had a considerable body of his own servants with him, whether slaves or employees (4:16; 5:10, 16). He was also able to keep open table at his own expense, without being a burden on the impoverished district of Judah (5:14–18). This enables us to understand better the dilemma of Sanballat, the governor of Samaria, and his advisers, Tobiah and Geshem.

Until Nehemiah's coming Sanballat's power extended almost certainly over Judea as well. It follows that Nehemiah must have been given the position of Tirshatha, or governor, before he started his journey. It was clear to Sanballat that Nehemiah was a rich and influential courtier, for the time being at least high in the king's favour. At the same time he did not know exactly what powers he might have been given, and Nehemiah took good care not to let him know. So Sanballat did not really venture to try and stop him in case he was acting within his instructions, and he did not dare to denounce him, lest trying to hurt a royal favourite might rebound and harm him. It had been easier for him, when the walls had first been repaired. Whoever "the Jews that came up from you" (Ezr. 4:12) may have been, they evidently did not create as imposing an effect as Nehemiah.

We can no longer identify the line of walls described in 2:13–15 with any certainty. Until recently it was assumed that the walls of Jerusalem under the later monarchy coincided, except perhaps in the north, with those in the time of Christ. It followed that this would have been the line followed by Nehemiah also. Today the opinion is gradually winning its way, that at least in the south monarchical Jerusalem never crossed the Central Valley to what is now called Mt. Zion. If that is so, and I am personally convinced that the view is correct, Nehemiah was concerned only with the eastern hills of Ophel, Zion and Moriah, with perhaps an extension to the north-west. Excavations have shown that the Babylonian destruction had been so thorough that Nehemiah, or more likely his unfortunate predecessors, was not able to follow the original line of Jebusite and Davidic fortifications, but had to build higher up the slopes of Ophel.*

The first reaction of Sanballat and his counsellors was to suggest rebellion (2:19). Since Nehemiah was a royal favourite, this was in itself absurd, but they hoped that he would produce his permission from the king, and this would give them some idea how they might react. Nehemiah's answer was that the building was religious in nature and therefore was of no concern to the Samaritans.

The Jews were far too poor to hire professional stonemasons. Nehemiah decided that the best guarantee of honest work would be to let the wealthier houseowners and their clients work on those sections of the wall that guaranteed their own safety. Those who were not directly involved were allocated the remaining stretches. This will also have minimized the dislike of many of the free farmers to taking orders and have introduced a healthy sense of rivalry between group and group. It should be noted that none of those mentioned as having come to Jerusalem with Ezra (Ezr. 8:1–14) seem to have taken any part in the rebuilding. For the implications of this fact see Additional Note.

There were influential families in Jerusalem, whom we shall meet later, who were on the best of terms with the leading families in Samaria. There were also not a few who had lost face over the disastrous earlier attempt to rebuild the walls. So when Sanballat and Tobiah mocked the new attempt (4:2f.), it was intended to drive a wedge between these people and Nehemiah. His intense anger is an indication of its considerable success (4:4f.). It is clear that the text of 4:2 is corrupt, though it cannot be reconstructed with any certainty. At any rate we can be sure that "Will they sacrifice?" is out of place, for there is no evidence that the sacrifices had been interrupted, even when the rebuilding of the walls had been stopped.

The failure of the mockery made Sanballat and his allies realize that drastic measures were called for. The Persian authorities did not permit local fighting, but the distances, even within the satrapies, were so great, that anyone able to carry out a sudden stroke might hope to have the *fait accompli* accepted by the higher powers. If Sanballat could destroy Nehemiah's work more or less overnight, then the satrap of Beyond-the-River might well acquiesce, the more so as he or his predecessor had probably approved of the accusation of Ezr. 4:11–16.

This explains their plot (4:7, 8). It might serve to frighten the Jews (4:11), or they might catch them unawares. Fortunately, Nehemiah was able to obtain information about their plans from Jews living in the border districts (4:12). So whenever their forces drew near to Jerusalem, they found the people under

* Kathleen M. Kenyon, *Jerusalem*, pp. 78–104, 107f.

arms, which destroyed any hope of the immediate success essential for their plan.

The only hope left to them was to strike at Nehemiah directly. Four times Sanballat and Geshem invited him to meet them somewhere in the plain of Ono. Ono lay in the coastal plain about six miles north of Lydda. From the time of Sennacherib's invasion in 701 B.C. it had become an area of special administration lying between the Assyrian provinces of Samaria and Philistia. This status had continued under the Babylonians and Persians. So, from one point of view, it was neutral ground for both sides. What they wanted to do we do not know. "But they intended to do me harm" (6:2) was not a Divine revelation given to Nehemiah, but his interpretation of the situation. They may very well have won over the Persian representative in Ono to their side. There was after all, apart from hurt dignity, nothing to prevent their visiting Nehemiah in Jerusalem. Finally they had to fall back on veiled threats of denunciation to the Persian king (6:6–7).

Their last weapon was bribery. The prophets had not quite reached the stage depicted in Zech. 13:2–6, but they had fallen on such evil days that they were glad to accept payment for prophesying against Nehemiah's policy. The words of Noadiah and the rest seem to have been too crude to call for further description (6:14), but Shemaiah's attempt was more subtle. He was a man of good family, as is shown by his grandfather's name being mentioned as well as his father's. On the excuse that he was not able to go out—"who was shut up" (6:10)—he invited Nehemiah to come and visit him. When he did so, he was greeted with a prophetic "oracle" that there was a plot to assassinate him at night, and that he should take refuge in the Temple. Shemaiah would accompany him, though no reasons were given why he should do so (6:10). He may well have been a priest or Levite. When we realize that the temple complex had its own walls and gates, though not of a nature to arouse suspicion, there is no reason for supposing that it was a suggestion that Nehemiah should take refuge in the sanctuary itself. Nothing in Nehemiah's answer supports this, and it would have been intrinsically so absurd, that there was no hope that it would catch him.

Nehemiah answered, "Should such a man as I flee?". He meant that he would lose all respect as governor, if he were to run away from a threat of this kind. Then he added, "And what man such as I could go into the temple and live?". Evidently there was a further obstacle which did not affect everyone. The simplest explanation is that Nehemiah was a eunuch and thereby debarred from the temple area (Deut. 23:1). By following what claimed to be a Divine oracle Nehemiah would have put himself in a position where he would lose all influence. His official position might have saved him from punishment, but any claim to be acting in God's name would have lost all hope of being believed. We must always beware of so-called guidance which flies in the face of God's clear revelation.

Mockery, intimidation, treachery and false oracles had all failed. In the incredibly short time of fifty-two days the work was finished (6:15). The minimum length we can ascribe to the finished wall is 4000 yards, or nearly two and a half miles. Even if we make full allowance for the fact that it was more repair than new building, and that many of the stones previously used had been left lying about, cf. 4:2, it was a prodigious effort. We can understand the workmen's complaint, as they sang,

> "The burden-bearers' strength is failing;
> the rubble is so very much;
> we are not sufficient
> to build up the wall" (4:10).

Something of the stress and strain may be seen in the fact that Nehemiah, though he was accustomed to the fastidious cleanliness of the Persian court, did not even undress at night or change his clothes.

Great must have been the rejoicing, when the day of dedication came. It began with purification ceremonies of an unspecified nature (12:30). These were followed by a great procession along the walls. The people were divided into two groups. Starting at the south end of the city they marched to the sound of psalms, one group along the east wall and the other along the west wall, until they met again at the Temple, where the festivities were continued.

Though no political advantage followed, and shortly after Nehemiah's time we find a Persian, Bagoas, as governor, the Jews in their dispersion now had not merely a religious but also a political centre. How far this was an advantage is a question that must wait until we have all the facts before us.

Nehemiah the Social Reformer

Since Nehemiah's building work was finished in the first half of September (6:15), it must have been begun in July immediately after the cereal harvest had been brought in but before most of the summer fruits were ripe. To the hard work were added the stress and strain of outside threats, the summer heat and the attempts to rescue the fruit harvest as well. It was apparently the women who broke down first and revealed social conditions that Nehemiah had never guessed (5:1).

There seem to have been three groups of persons principally involved. There were the proletariat (5:2), who long before had lost their land. Indeed it is not improbable that this loss had taken place before the fall of the monarchy and had never been reversed at the return from Babylonia, cf. p. 11. Since the work on the walls was unpaid, it was the last straw. They were selling their sons and daughters as slaves so as to buy corn to keep themselves alive—the Hebrew text has been corrupted, cf. NEB. Then there were those who had been hit by the recent drought and had had to mortgage their fields (5:3). Their supplies were running out and they saw that they were in danger of having to follow the example of the first group. The third group was only starting on the slippery downward slope; they had been hard hit by taxation demands, but they knew that once they were in debt there would be little chance of saving themselves (5:4). The chief fear of all of them was for their children.

There was a vicious circle involved. The small farmers had not been hit only by the droughts, for when they had exhausted their stores, they found that the cost of grain had shot up. The hoarders and profiteers who then lent them money to buy food then foreclosed on the farms, or on the children, if there was no ground left. All this was perfectly legal, though the Law of Moses had sought to remove the inhumanity from it. Its regulations, if carried out, would have prevented the development of any large slave population or of a large landless proletariat, but could not prevent much suffering in the short term. The rich doubtless pleaded their heavy losses, when the walls of Jerusalem had been thrown down again.

When Nehemiah first arrived, he was too concerned with his main purpose to realize how serious the economic position was. As a result he and those who had come with him had lent money and grain to those who had turned to them, probably in the hope that those from outside might be more humane than the rich of Jerusalem (5:10). After due deliberation he called the nobles and officials together and tried to make them realize what they had been doing (5:6). This was obviously without effect, so he called a general meeting of the people.

He pointed out a paradox to them. The Jews of the Eastern dispersion in Babylonia and Persia tried, so far they were able, to buy back and set free any Jewish slaves they heard of. This laudable practice remained for many centuries a first call on Synagogue funds. But here in Judea men were being sold as slaves, whom his friends at home would later have to buy back. To this those responsible could find no answer.

Nehemiah then acknowledged that he and his companions were not without blame in the matter. They would set the example which he urged them to follow, viz. the return of the pledges taken, whether lands, houses or persons, and a remission of the actual debt. The details have been blurred by the rendering of RV, RSV. Nehemiah did not accuse them of taking interest, which was illegal, but of laying a burden on them (see vv. 7, 10) by the taking of these pledges. Then it was not a question of a hundredth (5:11) but of the debt as a whole. NEB renders, "You are holding your fellow-Jews as pledges for debt (v. 7) . . . Let us give up this taking of persons as pledges for debt (v. 10) . . . their olive-groves and houses, as well as the income in money, and in corn, new wine, and oil" (v. 11). The rendering of JB is essentially the same. The chief creditors were unmoved when they met Nehemiah in a small group, but in front of the people as a whole, especially after the governor had set an example, the desire to keep a good name in public forced their hand.

There are loans which are a pure matter of convenience, and little, if anything, can be urged against them. Other loans are intended to facilitate purchases which can always be easily turned into cash once again. Once again there is little objection that can be raised. But where the loan is for daily bread and the clothing needed, if one is to do one's work, the borrower is in a very serious position. His optimism tells him that there is a better day coming, but it does not always come. Even if he does not have to pay interest, the loan becomes an ever heavier burden, dragging him down and down. Worst of all is if he has to pledge his land or the tools of his trade, for thereby he has mortgaged the future as well as the present. The Biblical ideal is that one should give and not lend in all these and similar cases.

Nehemiah's initiative could have led to a really new social beginning, but the rich had acted under pressure and not from conviction. For the moment Nehemiah had drawn the community sufficiently closely together to enable it to survive the storms that were threatening it, but even though he reinforced his plea by his constant example as long as he remained governor (5:14–18), there grew up an ever widening gap between rich and poor that was to bear very bitter fruit in the future.

He was soon to realize that he had not been forgiven by the rich. In 6:17–19 we read of the treacherous relations of many of the nobles with the Samaritan leaders. The oath of v. 18 probably refers to business dealings, for it can hardly have anything to do directly with marriage links.

The Repeopling of Jerusalem

The use of "city" in our standard translations of the Old Testament is highly misleading, for the settlements so entitled had only this in common, that they were fortified. Many of them by our modern concepts would have been villages; few were towns or even cities. As has been the case with us until fairly recently, there was a real difference in the nature of village and town life.

In Babylonia most of the exiles must have earned their living by working on the land or as artisans. It is true that we know of the Jewish bankers or money lenders, the Murashu family in Nippur in Babylonia,* but they probably started their business after the return of the exiles under Zerubbabel, i.e. under non-exilic conditions. As a result only a relatively small proportion of those who returned had any special interest in settling in Jerusalem. The damage done to the houses there had been greater, and so the task of rebuilding would be the harder. It was mainly those who had links with the Temple, the higher priestly families, the goldsmiths and perfumers, and those involved in administration that settled there.

So long as Jerusalem consisted mainly of strongly built aristocratic houses, it mattered little whether they were many or few, close together or scattered. Once the walls had been rebuilt, there had to be sufficient men in the city to man them. Indeed, at first Nehemiah had to take stringent precautions to guard against a sudden raid, especially at dawn and dusk (7:1–4). The heads of the various more important families soon moved to Jerusalem, if they were not there already (11:1, 3). Some, seeing the need, moved there of their own free will (11:2). For the rest lots had to be cast so as to bring up the population to the required minimum, one-tenth of the complete population.

We know from New Testament times something of the very great poverty that existed in Jerusalem alongside very great riches. It may well be that Nehemiah's efforts artificially to establish the city had much to do with this. Under the Persian rule trade to and from Egypt went mostly by sea via the Phoenician ports. So there will not even have been much trade to enrich the city up among the hills.

Most of the accounts of the ordering of the Temple personnel are clearly not

* Cf. DOTT, pp. 95f.

taken from Nehemiah's Memoirs, so we cannot know how much part he took in this work. The probability is that he kept himself clear of it. First of all he was a layman, and probably one excluded from the Temple worship at that. Secondly, he would not wish to create a precedent, which might allow a later Persian governor to interfere with the ordering of the Temple administration. Probably he confined himself to the everyday routine of government.

Then after twelve years he returned to the royal court (5:14; 13:6). No indication is given why he should do so. Some have suggested that he could see problems looming up, which he did not consider himself competent to deal with. It may be that one of the many accusations made by his enemies had raised suspicion, and he had to go and answer charges laid against him. It may have been simply for business and personal reasons. Be it as it may, it is clear that as soon as he had gone, most of the abuses he had kept down with a strong hand broke loose.

Nehemiah's Second Governorship

Since we do not know why Nehemiah returned to Artaxerxes, we can have no certain idea when he came back. The completely vague phrase, "after some time" (13:6), which should not be interpreted of too brief a period, suggests that his return had been more than merely a routine leave.

The course of events is not too clear, because we cannot date "on that day" (13:1). It cannot refer to the hallowing of the walls, for Eliashib's desecration of the Temple had taken place before "that day" (13:4). Had it happened as early as all this, Nehemiah would have dealt with the trouble at once.

So much is clear. Eliashib, the high priest (3:1), had a grandson who was Sanballat's son-in-law (13:28). It is probable that Tobiah was also connected with Sanballat by marriage. Hence there was some link between Eliashib and Tobiah, which is not given more closely in 13:4. The high priest placed a large room in the Temple courts at the disposal of his relative in law. This may suggest that the Ammonite was actually being admitted to the worship of Jehovah.

The day came, however, when the people realized that Ammonites were among those who had no place in Israel's worship (13:1-3). They accepted the law, apparently without dissent, but the high priest shrugged it off. There was very little or nothing that the people could do to influence a high priest, if he decided to ignore the law. It was only after a very bitter struggle that the Pharisees were later able to enforce some of their views on the Sadducean priests.

When Nehemiah returned, he very soon discovered what had happened; he brushed aside all precedents and protocol. Though very often the actions done at the command of a highly placed person are so expressed that one might think that he had done it personally, here, however, it is highly probable that Nehemiah did some of the throwing out with his own hands. We are reminded of our Lord's cleansing of the Temple, and then too the flaming anger of the one who acted gagged any protest by upset ecclesiastics.

There are probably many Christians who, in theory at least, agree that tithing is a wise and proper activity, but who fall far short of their ideal. Effective tithing calls for careful organization, and it may be bookkeeping. There are no indications that Nehemiah's contemporaries objected in principle to the paying of tithes, but without an effective organization much would be overlooked. Then, when they were brought in, their distribution would be largely in the hands of the priests. With a high priest like Eliashib, there would be little zeal for fair dealing among his subordinates, so the Levites and Temple singers had abandoned their duties in order to till their own fields. It is true that the priests were also among the losers, but they had also income from the sacrifices. This too Nehemiah put right, apparently without any protests from the Temple authorities. This shows to what extent he had increased in stature in the course of the years.

Laxity in the sanctuary was inevitably accompanied by laxity in everyday life, and this in turn was quite obviously shown in the way the Sabbath was kept. For the countryman there is always one particular temptation. Though nature normally knows little of the rush that marks our city life, there comes the moment, generally in harvest, when all its powers seem to unite in one great spate. Then it seems to man that he must work while he can. That is what Nehemiah saw happening (13:15). The other thing was an example of normal human logic. The farmers round Jerusalem came up to the city for the Temple-worship on the Sabbath, for the Pharisaic concept of the Sabbath-day's journey had not yet been introduced. In addition, whatever the history of the Synagogue, it must be regarded as virtually certain that it played no part in Judea at this time. So it seemed only fitting and right to them that they should combine religion and profit, first the worship and then the market, and to the citizens of Jerusalem it seemed right also. So well known had the Jerusalem Sabbath market become that traders came from afar to it. Nehemiah had no time for "ifs and buts" but made an end of it all with a high hand.

As he went round the streets of Jerusalem to see what else might have happened while he was away, he was struck by the number of children playing in the streets who did not seem to be able to speak Hebrew. He soon discovered that these were the children of mixed marriages. The important thing was not that they spoke their mothers' languages, but that they had not learnt Hebrew (13:23f.).

In our modern world it is normally regarded as a sign of a reactionary mind, if one queries the wisdom of intermarriage. It is, however, God's will that a marriage should result in a new unity, a unity which demands a certain amount of renunciation on both sides. Far too often this is found to be too big a price to pay, once the first flush of love is past. This was the case with some of these mixed marriages in Jerusalem. These foreign women may or may not have accepted the religion of their husbands, but their hearts were still in their old homes. As a result their children, when they grew a little older, would find themselves torn between two societies and feel themselves at home in neither.

Nehemiah, unlike Ezra, was not moved by any general religious theories. He was influenced by practical considerations, and the very real religious danger involved. At the same time, as a practical man of the world, he did not try Ezra's exaggerated methods of dissolving marriages, some of which may have existed for a considerable time. That which was had to remain, but he tried to ensure that intermarriage would cease. We are not told who those were whom he beat and mishandled (13:25), but they were probably rather the fathers of those who had contracted the marriages than the culprits themselves, for they would normally have approved and sometimes even actively favoured the mixed marriages, most of which will have been entered on for financial reasons (cf. Mal. 2:11, 13–16).

The most notorious case of mixed marriage was that of one of the high priest's grandsons, who had become son-in-law of Sanballat of Samaria (13:28). Evidently Nehemiah felt that a drastic example was called for and he banished him from Judah. He is very often identified with the Manasseh of whom Josephus tells in *Ant.* XI. vii. 2; viii. 1, 2, who became the first Zadokite high priest of the Samaritans. Josephus places the incident three generations later and makes no link with Nehemiah. On the other hand he is so notoriously unreliable for this period, that it is not impossible that it was for this banished priestling that Sanballat built the temple on Mt. Gerizim, cf. pp. 64–66.

While chs. 8–10 are certainly not part of Nehemiah's Memoirs, the absence of Ezra's name in ch. 10 strongly suggests that it should be separated from the two preceding chapters and be regarded as an agreement with the leaders of the people, which Nehemiah made after his drastic spring-cleaning on his return. Apart from Nehemiah himself and his secretary Zedekiah, it was signed by 21 priests, 17 Levites and 44 representatives of the people as a whole. It is remarkable that we do not have Eliashib's name, but closer inspection suggests that probably five and possibly all the priestly signatures are family names, Seraiah, cf. Ezr. 7:1, 2 Ki. 25:18, 1 Chr. 6:14f., representing the high priestly clan. In this way all the priests were committed by the heads of their clans. The names of the Levites are equally representative, as may be seen by comparing them with 8:7.

With two exceptions the points promised are just those that had particularly involved Nehemiah. There was the promise to avoid mixed marriages (10:28–30), Sabbath trading and the exacting of debts in the seventh year (10:31). There was the institution of a Temple tax, later to be raised from a third to half a shekel per annum and the organization of a wood offering. The fact that these are not earlier mentioned is no indication that they did not form part of Nehemiah's programme. Finally there was the organization of first-fruits and tithes, which we know to have been his concern.

In the East Nehemiah had accepted Ezra's ideals and interpretation of the Law. He did not have the spiritual standing to introduce them to or enforce them on the Judean community, but his practical wisdom created the setting in which they could flourish. Whatever some of the later effects of his measures, they did also create the setting in which the rabbinic understanding of the Law could be enforced and so Jewry gradually became the people of the Book.

His end is wrapped in silence. His tomb is not shown by tradition. The very brevity and misunderstanding in Josephus' account in the *Antiquities* shows that there were many who had no interest in keeping his memory green, while religiously he was outshone by Ezra. We do not know whether he died suddenly in office, worn out by his many labours, or whether he returned to a lonely and childless home in the East with only his deeds to keep his memory alive among men.

That the Chronicler did not incorporate Nehemiah's Memoirs in his history but only used them as a sort of appendix is easy to explain. His work was concerned mainly with the history of the Davidic monarchy and of the Temple. Since Nehemiah did not fit in directly with either, he had no clear place in the story. It is harder to explain why future tradition neglected him in contrast to its glorification of Ezra. The simplest explanation is that religious conformity is almost always easier for man than social righteousness. It was easy for the rich and mighty, whether priests or laity, to accept Ezra's interpretation and enforcement of the Law. Nehemiah on the other hand offended both the priests and the wealthy leaders of Jerusalem's society. They accepted the greater security and political importance which Nehemiah had procured for them, but they found it hard to forgive the unavoidably dictatorial methods by which they were secured.

ADDITIONAL NOTE

The Relationship of Ezra to Nehemiah

Most of the major controversies concerning the interpretation of the Old Testament have stemmed from *a priori* theories about revelation and prophecy. The problem of the relationship between Ezra and Nehemiah arises entirely from the Biblical evidence itself.

The evidence of Scripture itself seems quite simple. Ezra went to Jerusalem in the seventh year of Artaxerxes (Ezr. 7:7); Nehemiah returned in the twentieth year (Neh. 2:1). The implementation of Ezra's mission had apparently to wait until the coming of Nehemiah (Neh. 8), although he had acted vigorously about mixed marriages almost as soon as he had arrived in Judea (Ezr. 9, 10).

The denial by some extremer scholars that the royal instruction to Ezra (Ezr. 7:12–26) could possibly be genuine has led to a closer study of its terms. This has created an increasing willingness to accept it and so has brought a greater awareness of the problems inherent in the story. Put briefly the central one is that Ezra returned in 458 B.C. with full powers to enforce the Mosaic Law, yet he did so only in the governorship of Nehemiah (444 B.C.). The most popular and indeed the only cogent explanation is, to quote Stafford Wright's words about Ezra, "Although his commission did not extend to rebuilding, he was keen enough on the new wall to thank God for it in ix. 9. He need not have taken part in the building himself. But, when the enemies destroyed the new walls, Ezra's stock would fall immediately."* A theory based on no evidence can hardly be held to be convincing. The same applies to the suggestion that Ezra had returned after dealing with the mixed marriages (Ezr. 9, 10). Both theories fail to give due weight to the drastic powers given to Ezra (Ezr. 7:25, 26), which did not depend on popular acceptance.

Scholarly opinions have been strongly divided, the line of demarcation

* *The Date of Ezra's Coming to Jerusalem²* (1958).

having little to do with the traditional division of conservative and liberal. At first very many accepted the statement in Ezr. 7:7 that Ezra returned in the seventh year of Artaxerxes, but of Artaxerxes II, i.e. 398 B.C. Stafford Wright's argument in *The Date of Ezra's Coming to Jerusalem* has however, caused many to abandon this view. Most popular today is probably the view first put forward by Wellhausen that we should read "the twenty-seventh year" in Ezr. 7:7, i.e. 438 B.C. Rudolph argues that once a figure is accepted as corrupt there is no merit in playing around with it, and he puts Ezra's visit between Nehemiah's two governorships.* This view has received little approval but there is very much to be said for it.

When we come to the actual arguments taken from the text itself, they are remarkably unconvincing and most have been used by both sides. There is, however, one argument that has tilted the scales so far as I am concerned. With one doubtful exception none of those named as returning with Ezra is recorded as taking part in the rebuilding of the wall in Neh. 3. The one possible exception is Hattush (Ezr. 8:2, Neh. 3:10); when we compare these with 1 Chr. 3:22, we shall probably decide that it is purely the result of a fairly common name, cf. Neh. 12:2.

In fact the whole controversy is intrinsically of very little importance, for the two men, Ezra and Nehemiah, were essentially working for different ends, even if their religious outlook was identical. So they have been treated separately, and if desired the chapter on Ezra may be read before that on Nehemiah. Once it is realized that Nehemiah is essentially an appendix to Chronicles-Ezra, and that it is easy enough to identify Nehemiah's Memoirs, the arrangement suggested of Ezra's activities does no violence to the text.

Anyone wishing to immerse himself in the arguments pro and con can refer to H. H. Rowley, *The Chronological Order of Ezra and Nehemiah*, reprinted in *The Servant of the Lord*.

---

* *Esra und Nehemia* (HAT—1949).

EZRA

Though many priests returned with Joshua and Zerubbabel to Jerusalem, there were those that remained in Babylonia. Most maintained their priestly traditions, for it was possible for Herod to choose one of his high priests from there, cf. p. 112. The best known among them was Ezra. He is never presented to us as a functioning priest, though he may well have so acted, when he returned to Jerusalem. He is seen as "a scribe skilled in the law of Moses" (Ezr. 7:6) and also as "Ezra the priest, the scribe of the law of the God of heaven" (7:12). Formerly these two titles were taken as synonymous, the latter being used even as an argument against the authenticity of the decree of Artaxerxes (7:12–26). Today, in spite of their similarity, they are very generally recognized as distinct.

Ezra was a scribe skilled in the law of Moses. Though in Old Testament times the ability to read and write was commoner than was once thought, fluency was rare, due to lack of opportunity. Even a member of a priestly family like Jeremiah, who was probably educated in Jerusalem, used a scribe, Baruch, to write down his prophecies in a scroll (Jer. 36:4, 32). Not merely to keep the nation's records, but to know what was in them, called for high skill, and so the Scribe is a title we frequently meet for one of the highest officials of state under the monarchy, e.g. 2 Sam. 8:17; 20:25, 1 Ki. 4:3, 2 Ki. 18:18 (RSV "secretary", NEB "adjutant-general"). What was necessary in the national realm, must early have been in the religious one as well. We may affirm with certainty that the Babylonian exile made it an absolute necessity that someone should be responsible for the preservation of the people's sacred records.

A scribe like Ezra was not simply responsible for the copying of the Scriptures; in one way that was the least of his responsibilities. He had to guarantee that the copies were accurate, which in turn virtually demanded his knowing the Scriptures, or at least the more important sections, off by heart, so that where the eye or ear was deceived the memory would not be. It was no mere feat of learning by heart. Means were devised by which the memory was aided in obtaining an intelligent grasp of the Scriptures. If the modern view is correct that many of the men of Qumran spent much of their time copying the Scriptures and other religious books, not merely for the community but also for sale outside, it shows what stress was laid on the work being done by suitable men. Such a one was Ezra.

He was also "the scribe of the law of the God of heaven". The Assyrians had left a great deal of political autonomy to their subject races, but they tried to ensure their political loyalty by a demand that they should include the gods of Assyria in their official worship. The Persians followed the opposite policy. Thanks to a much improved organization and civil service they were able to concede only the minimum of political freedom throughout their empire, but in exchange they gave complete religious freedom. Indeed they even insisted on the proper carrying out of the varying religious systems of the many subject nations, for they believed that this would help to ensure the welfare of the state. Earlier it was noted, cf. p. 23, that they, or at least the civil service department involved, could be concerned even with the religion of the Jews at the frontier-post at Elephantine, near Aswan in the south of Egypt.

It is now generally conceded that there was, to use modern terms, a Ministry for Religious Affairs in the Persian civil service, and that Ezra was one of the highest officials in the Jewish section, if not its head. As was pointed out in ch. 1 "the God of heaven" seems to have been the title the Jews themselves chose for Jehovah, when they had to deal with their polytheistic or Zoroastrian neighbours, and so it was also adopted in official circles. So much was this the case that Nehemiah uses it quite naturally (1 : 4f.; 2 : 4, 20); the absence of the title in the later portions of the book may perhaps be explained by his being in an almost purely Jewish setting. Ezra's official position is a sufficient explanation of the surprisingly wide range of powers entrusted to him.

The Decree of Artaxerxes

If we could date Ezra's return to Jerusalem with certainty, cf. the Additional Note to the previous chapter, it would make it easier to answer some of the problems connected with Artaxerxes' decree (7 : 12–26), but they are all of small importance. In addition our understanding of Ezra's work does not depend on our views of his relationship to Nehemiah.

Unlike Nehemiah, Ezra was apparently given no direct political power, but religiously his authority was limited only by the law of Moses, which he was to administer. It is clear from 7 : 14 that he had a copy of the Law, which had been approved by his "Ministry", where another copy must have been stored up. Indeed, we can assume without reasonable doubt, that it was already being enforced among the Jews of the eastern dispersion, in Babylonia and Persia. The "magistrates and judges" (7 : 25), whom Ezra was to appoint in the satrapy Beyond-the-River, which included Judea, would have authority only over Jews, and that in matters which the Persians considered to be outside their criminal law.

This is the first example of what we today call the "millet" system that has come down to us. It has existed in Palestine and in the Near-East ever since. It meant that every recognized religious community was given the right to regulate its own affairs and enforce its own internal religious laws, so long as they did not conflict with the laws of the sovereign state. In other words, what was implicit in Cyrus' permission for the return to build the Temple had now become explicit. Palestinian Jewry had become a religious body and was no longer a national state. The change of status was marked by the special privileges given to the religious functionaries (7 : 24). From now on the high priest

became the representative and real ruler of Judean Jewry, and this led to his becoming increasingly the head of Jewry at large.

There was nothing out of the ordinary in the state support for the public
cultus. We need only remember that according to Josephus the Jews offered
sacrifices twice every day for Caesar and the Roman people; from Philo we
know these had been paid for by Augustus. Though fighting had broken out
earlier, it was the ending of these sacrifices that made the rebellion against
Rome official.

Ezra's Return

Whatever may have been the intention of Artaxerxes and the "Ministry for
Religious Affairs", it is clear that Ezra had his own interpretation of things.
Though the best part of a century had passed since Cyrus' decree and the return
under Joshua and Zerubbabel, Ezra clearly regarded himself as the leader of the
true return, the fulfiller of Isaiah's prophecies. Perhaps he was encouraged in
such an idea by the way the earlier generation had been disappointed in its high
hopes.

The beginning of the return is dated as being on the first day of the first
month (7:9), which from the sequel seems clearly to have been Nisan, the
Passover month. This is significant only if we take it in conjunction with Ezra's
obvious determination to make the caravan representative of the whole
people.

In the list of those returning (8:1–14) we have a priestly group from each of
the main divisions of the priesthood (8:2ab). That Gershom and D. niel represent groups is shown by 8:24. If Ezra is not mentioned in the list, contrast
Zerubbabel and Jeshua in 2:2, it may well be because he was under obligation
to return to his post in the Persian capital. Then we have a member of the royal
family mentioned (8:2c). There follow the names of *twelve* families of com-
moners. Any last doubt of Ezra's desire that his caravan should represent all
Israel should be dispelled by his efforts to ensure the presence of Levites
(8:15–20).

The interpretive translation of RSV in v. 13, "Of the sons of Adonikam,
those who came later" (RV, "And of the sons of Adonikam, *that were* the
last"), is very misleading. It might suggest that they came in a later caravan,
which is certainly not intended, or it might be understood as distinguishing
them from earlier members of the family who returned under Zerubbabel
(2:13). The simplest rendering is that of NEB, "The last were the family of
Adonikam . . .", i.e. the list ended with them. It is this list that makes it so hard
to place Ezra's return before Nehemiah's first term as governor, for none of
those mentioned finds any certain place in the list of those that helped to
rebuild the walls (Neh. 3), cf. Additional Note to previous chapter.

It was his conviction that he was in some sense a new Moses that made Ezra
ashamed to ask the king for an armed guard (8:22). He could look back not
merely to the Exodus itself but also to Isaiah's prophecies of the new Exodus
with their record and promise of Divine protection. But the hard facts scared
him. There were, apart from an indefinite number of priests, fifteen named and

1511 unnamed laymen; then 38 Levites and 220 temple slaves were added to the total (8:18–20). When we add women and children we have to reckon with some 6,000 persons. The news of such a caravan would spread rapidly far and wide. The report of the treasure carried, quite apart from private property, must have travelled widely and lost nothing in the telling. In addition a journey of something over a hundred days (7:8; 8:31), often over difficult and broken ground, lay before them. It is not surprising then that the glow of en‍thusiasm that had filled his heart, when he was received by the king to be given his credentials, evaporated a little, when he was by the irrigation canal Ahava.

Hence, though it might not be physically the best preparation for a long trek, he called a fast, as did Esther, when she faced the greatest crisis of her life (Est. 4:16). God saw the humiliation and heard the prayers, and so the company reached its goal without loss or hurt.

Ezra's Activity

There must always remain a question mark over the exact details and timing of Ezra's activities. We must, however, always bear two things in mind. One is that by universal assent among those that can read Hebrew Neh. 7:73c–9:37 belongs to the story of Ezra and not to Nehemiah's Memoirs, however the story is, or is not, to be fitted into the story of Nehemiah.

The other is that Ezra was not simply an influential priest who had decided to return to the land of his fathers and who could take his time in convincing his people to take a serious interest in the Law as he understood it. He was a very high official in the Persian civil service; he had been given plenary powers by the king to act in matters of religion. Since his letter of authority was addressed to the Persian authorities in the satrapy Beyond-the-River (8:36), it is clear that he could have called on them, if there had been any effective opposition to his measures. Since it cannot be proved that he had to return home again, too much stress may not be laid upon this probability, but in any case any reconstruction of the position, which suggests his either ignoring his commission for years or doing what he was not authorized to do, should be adopted only as a last resort.

The purely administrative side of Ezra's task, viz. the appointment of magistrates and judges (7:25), is not mentioned, presumably because the historian assumed that the reader would take it for granted. Yet this was one of the most important parts of Ezra's reform and ensured its success. The two incidents that are recorded are the dissolution of mixed marriages (chs. 9, 10) and the reading of the Law (Neh. 8). When we look at the chronological details, we discover that the latter occurred in the seventh month (Neh. 7:73), the former in the ninth month (Ezr. 10:9), though in neither case is the year mentioned. They will be considered in this order, and we shall see that the logic of events will justify it. In fact the dissolution of the marriages, at least in its more dramatic features, is hardly comprehensible, unless we assume a prior knowledge of the Law of Moses.

To understand the nature and greatness of Ezra's achievement we need to obtain some idea of the part played by the Law of Moses, or Torah, before his day and above all before the exile. This is not the place to deal once again with the critical attack on the Mosaic authorship of the Pentateuch. It is irrelevant to our purpose. In addition the old critical positions tend today to be little more than the termite-eaten shells of old scholarly "orthodoxy". The increasing recognition of the antiquity of the material contained in the so-called sources makes these today little more than relics of man's ingenuity and scholarship.

Few, if any, today will suggest that the ordinary private person under the monarchy possessed his own personal copy of the Pentateuch in whole or part, the more so as the importance of oral transmission and teaching is increasingly being recognized. The Pentateuch itself often stresses the importance of a father's teaching his children, e.g. Gen. 18:19, Exod. 12:26f.; 13:8, 14, Deut. 4:9f.; 6:7, 20; 11:19; 32:46, cf. Josh. 4:6, 21. It is now generally agreed that such oral transmission, whether at home or in the wider community, formed a most important part of a growing lad's education. There were other ways also in which he learned the traditions of the past.

To the last, until the Jewish commonwealth was destroyed by the Romans, justice remained mainly a local matter, as indeed it is today among those Jews who still recognize the authority of the Rabbinic courts. It was carried out by the more influential citizens in the presence of any who chose to be present. While a greater degree of formality may have developed, down to the fall of the monarchy most court cases will have followed the pattern depicted in Ruth 4. In fact, though Jeremiah was being tried before the highest judges in the land (Jer. 26:7–19), the procedure was little, if any, different. Particularly interesting was the right shown there (vv. 17–19) for those who were able to quote precedents to reinforce or challenge the opinion of the judges. We do not find the prophets attacking incorrect law, where the law courts were concerned, but deliberate perversion of evidence and judgement and the force exercised by the rich. There is no reason for supposing that the basic law between man and man was ever in doubt, though its application might be affected by outstanding precedents, and as 1 Sam. 30:25 shows, those matters not covered by the Mosaic legislation could be settled by competent authority.

The basic religious law will have been repeated, along with the outstanding stories of God's actions in Israel's history, at the pilgrim feasts. This was expressly demanded in Deut. 31:10–13, where "this law" (it is not clear whether Deuteronomy, or the Pentateuch is intended) is to be read during Tabernacles every seventh year. While the modern scholar who believes that this became an annual event may or may not be correct, there can be no doubt that the week-long festivals of Passover and Tabernacles were partly spent in re-hearing at least the more important sections of the law.

What may be called social law, concerning clean and unclean, the permitted and forbidden in marriage, etc., will have been part of every boy's and girl's upbringing, and will have needed no further teaching. Only in matters of sacrifice, ceremonial cleansing, and the like, will the priests very largely have kept the detail of the Law secret. It was for them to decide how things should be done, but there is no evidence of frequent infringements of the ritual. The fate of Hophni and Phineas (1 Sam. 2:12–17; 4:11) will have served as a long remembered and salutary warning.

The prophets hardly ever mention sins of ignorance. They attack the deliberate contravention of the moral law, the deliberate perversion of justice, or the carrying out of ritual practices, like sacred prostitution or human sacrifice, which sprang from assimilating the worship of Jehovah to that of other gods. It is clear that they prophesied to people who knew, or ought to have known, what God expected of them.

When Josiah showed such consternation when the book of the law was read to him (2 Ki. 22 : 11), it is clear that it was its condemnation of idolatry that affected him, and it is affirmed by Huldah that this was the real sin (2 Ki. 22 : 17). There is no suggestion that the Law in its main demands was unknown to him.

Throughout the Old Testament period, however, we gain the impression that the average Israelite regarded the Torah of Moses, not as God's gracious instruction, but simply as we regard law. It concerned him only when he broke it, or was tempted to do so. Indeed, since it was not a democratic society, the responsibility for the keeping of much of the law lay on the leaders of the people. Note that no condemnation of the elders of Jezreel for the judicial murder of Naboth is uttered by either Elijah or the Scriptures. They were merely carrying out instructions, and the responsibility lay upon Ahab and Jezebel. Even more striking is the way Jeremiah discounts the behaviour of the ordinary Jerusalem citizen (Jer. 5 : 4). He could not be expected to behave any better than the great and powerful.

Today the religious Jew insists that Torah should be rendered Instruction, not Law. In this he is completely correct, but since God's instruction in detail will always have the force of law, if taken seriously, there has always been the tendency so to regard it. When Paul used the term "law" (*nomos*), he was merely following the usage of the Alexandrian Synagogue enshrined in the LXX. It should, however, be noted that we generally think of law in terms of Common or Statute Law, while this use is probably not to be found in the N.T. at all. Where it is not used of the Mosaic Law, it generally applies to general principles or norms.

Even in the cultus, though the ordinary citizen was expected to play his part, the main stress lay on the king. Just as Bethel could be called "the king's sanctuary" (Amos 7 : 13), so clearly the king was supreme in all but priestly functions in the Jerusalem sanctuary. We need hardly be surprised that there were so many "nonconformists", people who preferred the homely atmosphere and lack of pomp of the local "high place" to the impersonality, glitter and pomp of the official sanctuaries.

What Ezra did was to impress on the people that the Torah of Moses was addressed to each of them individually and not merely to their leaders, and that however many laws it might contain it was primarily instruction. By getting this across he was able to change the whole outlook of the Jewish people and to leave a mark on them that has not been lost to this day.

Ezra and the Torah

Ezra arrived in Jerusalem on the first day of Ab, i.e. sometime in August. After three days of rest he handed over all the gifts for the Temple, and those who had come with him settled down in their new homes. The fruit harvest had not been fully brought in yet, so Ezra did not hasten matters, though he will have talked over ways and means at least with those who were sympathetic with his mission.

On the first of Tishri the people gathered in great expectation (Neh. 8:1). Even if Ezra had not said much about his purpose, he will have known how to leak as much as he wanted to, and his travelling companions will have made no secret about the purpose of his visit. It was the feast of Trumpets (Num. 29:1) and doubtless already the beginning of the civil year, though there is no indication that the later concepts of Rosh Hashanah (the Jewish New Year) had yet gathered round it. On the other hand the concept held under the monarchy that it might usher in the Day of the Lord had almost certainly not been forgotten. Nothing is said to suggest that Ezra saw anything special in the date, beyond its suitability as a public holiday, for the first of Nisan was still the real New Year's day for him, cf. p. 43 and Exod. 12:2.

We must stress, however, that the choice of meeting place was deliberate. It was in the square before the Water Gate. From Neh. 3:26 it is clear that this gate was not one of the city gates. It was evidently one that had led from the former royal palace, which had stood south of the Temple. Today its site will lie under the Herodian extension of the temple area. It was near enough to the Temple to allow attendance at the morning sacrifices, but since it was not sacred ground, women, the ritually unclean, and even those who for one reason or another were excluded from the religious community of Israel and its worship could attend.

In the choice of site we have Ezra's deliberate proclamation that the Torah was greater than the Temple and its sacrifices, indeed that the Torah as such was above anything it might contain. Since nothing is said of the thirteen men who supported him (Neh. 8:4), the only legitimate assumption is that they were neither priests nor Levites, but laymen, heads of fathers' houses among the people. We might be tempted to reduce the thirteen names, some difficult, cf. the parallel list in 1 Esd. 9:43, 44, to twelve and so see in them representatives of "all Israel", were it not that here and in 1 Esd. 9:48 we have thirteen Levites to help him (8:7). He probably simply accepted the fact that there were thirteen outstanding elders and balanced them with thirteen Levites as his active helpers—Levites, for according to the Law teaching was one of their main functions.

This does not mean that the priests had been ignored, cf. 8:13; they had exercised their functions as the first act of worship that day. In addition the very stress on the Torah as a whole would automatically increase their importance. Ezra did not wish to give the impression that his mission was merely a priestly scheme—we must not forget that he was a priest himself.

There is no suggestion that this was a covenant-making ceremony, a presenting of a law to the people which they might accept or refuse. In the first place it was "the law of the God of heaven" (Ezr. 7:12), which, as we saw earlier, was accepted by the Persian authorities as binding on the Jews. Then it does not fit into the considerable line of covenant-renewal ceremonies in Judah's history. However we interpret 9 : 38 (Heb. 10 : 1), it refers to certain definite commands which the people promised to keep. On any interpretation it refers to something that cannot have taken place until some weeks later, cf. 9 : 1 and the exegesis below. Finally, there is no suggestion of acceptance or rejection. The people had recognized it as the Law of Moses in advance (8 : 1); it was simply a fact to which they could react with joy or sorrow.

The reading on the second day (8 : 13) was confined to the leaders of the people and the Temple personnel, because it was no public holiday; the adding of a second day to the Rosh Hashanah holiday came much later. This reinforces the impression made by the account of the first day's reading. Ezra had about five hours at his disposal (8 : 3), and even without translation he could not possibly have read the whole Pentateuch in that time. Indeed, if those scholars were correct who say it was only the "Priestly Code", he would not have been able to cover even that. In fact we are told that Ezra and the Levites read from the scroll (8 : 3, 8); in other words he chose such portions as he considered most apposite for the people.

Five hours meant a long session, especially as there were older children present (8 : 3). It would have been intolerable, had it not been broken up by translation (v. 8, RV, RSV, NEB margins) and explanation. The translation was, it need hardly be added, into Aramaic. The statement that the people remained in their places suggests that the Levites divided the crowd among them, explaining the difficulties felt in each section, which would undoubtedly vary from group to group.

The immediate reaction of the people was tears, for the most part probably for sins of omission rather than commission. Had it been otherwise, it is hard to conceive of even the most legalistic of men, a charge that can hardly be made against Ezra, demanding feasting because it was a festival, the feast of Trumpets, and the leaving of confession, contrition and restitution until after sundown. It was their joy in the Lord that had moved them to tears, when they realized that they had fallen short of His will. Ezra reassured them that the very fact that they joyed in Him was a guarantee of His safe-keeping. The festal food had, of course, been prepared in any case. The "portions" were to be sent to those who were too poor to have prepared anything special. The Synagogue has always inculcated the privilege of having a guest at the Sabbath or festival table, whether a stranger or a local poor man. Here, however, there were whole families unable to celebrate such a day as was fitting.

Suddenly we find the apparent sorrow transformed into great rejoicing, not by an effort of will, but "because they had understood the words that were declared to them" (v. 12). Surely this does not mean merely that the long hallowed words had been rendered into Aramaic. There is no indication that at this early date a significant portion of the population no longer spoke Hebrew—Neh. 12 : 24 seems to be conclusive on this point. It was not even that the Pentateuch, as we may see by comparing its language with that of Chronicles, was, like the English Authorised Version, in a language no longer appreciated by the man in the street. It was quite simply that these old commandments had suddenly become something addressed to them. They were no longer merely automatically to keep some old traditions or imitate the practices of their neighbours. God had spoken to them and they had understood it.

The first effect of the presentation of the Law was the celebrating of Tabernacles in a new way (8 : 17). We must understand "for from the days of Joshua the son of Nun to that day the people of Israel had not done so" in the light of 2 Ki. 23 : 23, 24, 2 Chr. 30 : 26. There is no suggestion that the feast had not been kept, indeed we know that it had, but now there was a new quality about it. The mention of what were essentially public booths, "in the courts of the house of God, and in the square at the Water Gate and in the square at the Gate of Ephraim" (8 : 16), suggests that they were for the pilgrims from the country. Evidently this was the first time that Tabernacles was centred on Jerusalem alone. There is no doubt that under the monarchy Tabernacles was the great popular festival, but it was celebrated to a great extent at local sanctuaries.

Ezra and Mixed Marriages

Doubtless Ezra and his "magistrates and judges" had many a clash with those whose practices were challenged by the law he was enforcing. One point, however, stood out, and when we study it, we shall see more clearly what Ezra was aiming at.

A couple of months after the reading of the Law, cf. Ezr. 10 : 9, the high officials came to Ezra with a report (9 : 1). The translation of *sar* by prince in pre-exilic settings is misleading enough; in the time of Ezra (so AV, RV) it is meaningless. We are not told who they were. It is quite probable that they were some of the judges he had appointed, for they should probably be differentiated from those mentioned in v. 2. The apparent publicity of their report and its sequel makes it likely that Ezra had instructed them to find out how the land lay.

In distinctly exaggerated terms they suggested that the community had rushed like the Gadarene swine to destruction, that they, led by their principal men, were indulging in wide-spread mixed marriages. That it was a wild exaggeration is shown by the list of the guilty in 10 : 18–43. In all 113 are mentioned, which means less than 1% of all marriages. Should it be argued that only the more important are named, which intrinsically is quite possible, experience shows us that in normal times such marriages are always more likely among the rich, who have more chance to meet foreigners and more to gain by marrying them. So it is reasonable to think that our list gives us a fair picture of what had happened. In any case it is a common experience that the extent of such practices almost always tends to be exaggerated.

We saw earlier that Nehemiah was influenced by practical and valid reasons in attacking mixed marriages; Malachi had shown that behind some of them lay deep selfishness; here a new note creeps in. We are not in a position to judge these marriages. Some may well have been downright disastrous; others may have been entered on for the worst motives; in some cases the wife may have brought all her heathen practices with her. But none of these things are alleged.

Ezra's confession concerned itself only with the fact that the law had been broken (9 : 10–15), and there is no suggestion that the commission (10 : 16) was concerned with anything but the bare fact. In addition the officials used an expression they had probably learnt from Ezra himself, "the holy seed has mixed itself with the peoples of the lands" (9 : 2), cf. Isa. 6 : 13.

It is, of course, possible, that no more than "the remnant" was intended, cf. 9 : 14, 15, but this is doubtful. It must be remembered that the attitude of Judaism towards proselytes has always been ambivalent. Under favourable conditions they have been welcome, and at some periods actively sought.* On the other hand there has always been a tendency to suspect them. The most striking modern example was the strong protests of the Naturei Karta in Jerusalem, when their leader, Rabbi Blau, married a proselyte of long and impeccable standing. Their children have always been accepted without question, but all too often the convert has felt that in some way he was an outsider. When John the Baptist said to the Pharisees and Sadducees, "God is able from these stones to raise up children to Abraham" (Matt. 3 : 9), he was putting his finger on an underlying tendency. Ezra did not see the remnant in Judea merely as the bearers of a faith and the continuers of the covenant, but also as the physical continuation of the people of the covenant. It is to this, however much or little he was conscious of it, that we must attribute the drastic and to some extent inhuman treatment of these mixed marriages.

Obviously we cannot be certain, but the considerable number of sympathizers with Ezra's views who were present (9 : 4; 10 : 1) suggests that rumours had been allowed to circulate that something was going to happen. If that is so, the proposal made by Shecaniah ben Jehiel (10 : 2–4) had probably been arranged beforehand. The vigorous terms in which the people were summoned to Jerusalem show how great and real the powers were that had been entrusted to Ezra as the king's representative.

One of the few things he could not control was the weather (10 : 9). Since he had come from Babylonia, he probably had little idea of what Palestinian winter rain could be like. We cannot guess the real feelings of his hearers. They challenged neither the facts nor Ezra's authority (10 : 12). They need not have been sympathetic towards the culprits, but they were not going to be pushed. The officials of verse 14 (*sarim*) were chosen by Ezra (v. 16) and were probably in part the same as those of 9 : 1. The people demanded that those who were guilty should be given the chance of confessing their fault, for they wanted neither denunciations nor snooping into family matters. Then they demanded that those involved might be accompanied by the local elders and judges, who would know their family circumstances.

Even so there were a few who had courage enough to oppose the whole procedure. We know nothing of the two laymen, Jonathan and Jahzeiah (10 : 15), except that they were not personally guilty and no obvious relatives are mentioned in 10 : 18–43. From Ezr. 8 : 16, Neh. 11 : 16, it is clear that their two sup-

---

* cf. Matt. 23 : 15. Their number cannot be established, but M. Grant, *The Jews in the Roman World*, pp. 60f., estimates that in the time of Julius Caesar 20% of the inhabitants of Rome's eastern provinces were Jews.

porters, Meshullam and Shabbethai, were of the highest standing.* Since their opposition is given us almost in brackets, as a virtual irrelevance, we cannot even guess the reasons they gave for opposing Ezra.

The two months needed for what was in essence a very simple task (10:16, 17) may have been due to the investigators' distaste for their task. It could have been caused by severe weather. In some cases the delay may have been used quietly to arrange a divorce, so that the culprits' names would not become known. In any case, before Passover came round, the whole matter had been settled.

The story ends with the strange statement, "some of the wives had borne children" (so margin of AV, RV). RSV, NEB are almost certainly correct in following the parallel account in 1 Esd. 9:36 and rendering "and they put them away with their children". *The Encyclopedia of the Jewish Religion* (p. 211b) states, "The origin of the rule that the child born of a Jewish father and a non-Jewish mother is not considered a Jew is obscure, but scriptural authority is adduced from Neh. 10:29 (*sic!*, presumably Ezr. 10), where it is said that Ezra obliged those Jews who had married foreign wives to put them away together with their children". We may take it that this was in fact the beginning of the formal ruling.

Solemn Repentance

Our exegesis has been based thus far on the supposition that Ezr. 9, 10 in fact follows on Neh. 8. If that is so, then the story of the mixed marriages is rounded off by the account in Neh. 9:1–37. Our normal lack of familiarity with the Jewish festal calendar hides from us the difficulty presented by Neh. 9:1. If we take it as the sequel to Neh. 8, it demands that immediately after the rejoicing of Tabernacles with an interval of only one day the people had to return to Jerusalem for a major fast, and that in spite of the Day of Atonement, which had taken place only a few days before Tabernacles. In addition no reason for the fast is offered. Once, however, we place it after Ezr. 10, there is no difficulty in seeing in the ceremony the solemn climax to the purging of foreign elements from Israel. The actual sending away of the foreign wives and their children needed a little time, and so the concluding ceremony was postponed until after Passover.

Ezra was a wiser administrator than he is sometimes given credit for being, and he knew how to strike when the iron was hot. "The Israelites separated themselves from all foreigners" (9:2) is not merely suggesting that they turned away those foreigners who wanted to take part in their fast, and it certainly implies more than the sending away of the unfortunate foreign wives and their children. Ezra was making it virtually impossible for such marriages to be repeated. While the phrase may imply the expulsion of some few non-Jews who had no legal right to live in Judea, it means mainly the withdrawal of all voluntary contacts with non-Jews. Ezra's powers did not cover any but his own people. Implied here is the beginning of those laws of social life, which were effectually to isolate Jewry from its heathen surroundings. Though Galilee was

* This assumes that Meshullam was the one mentioned in Ezr. 8:16, but it was a common name.

largely Gentile in the first century of our era, the only Gentile specifically mentioned as coming into contact with Jesus was the centurion of Matt. 8:5–13,
Lk. 7:1–10—the royal official of Jn. 4:46–53 need not have been a Gentile,
and the Syro-Phoenician woman lived already in "the district of Tyre and
Sidon" (Matt. 15:21). This is some indication of how complete the division
had become in Palestine. Whether the Greeks of Jn. 12:20 were Gentiles, as is
generally assumed, or Greek-speaking Jews, as maintained by some, they were
at the worst, from the Jewish point of view, semi-proselytes, else they would
not have come to Jerusalem for the Passover. The usual Jewish position is given
by Peter's words to Cornelius, and the attack made on him, when he returned
to Jerusalem (Acts 10:28; 11:3). It should be noted that the rigorists in Jerusalem were apparently not disturbed by Cornelius' baptism, but by "You have
been visiting men who are uncircumcised and sitting at table with them"
(NEB).

The Extended Torah

Ezra finished his great confession on the fast day with the words, "Behold we
are slaves this day; in the land that Thou gavest to our fathers to enjoy its fruit
and its good gifts, behold, we are slaves. And its rich yield goes to the kings
whom Thou has set over us because of our sins; they have power also over our
bodies and over our cattle at their pleasure, and we are in great distress" (Neh.
9:36, 37). Here we have the great problem that faced those that had returned
from Babylonia.

Idolatry was now a thing of the past. There is little evidence for any major
social injustice after Nehemiah's reforms until much later. Jehovah had shown
His power by restoring them to their home land, and yet they were not masters
in their own house. Even the extent of Ezra's religious authority only underlined the complete absence of political independence. Sin could be the only explanation, and the only adequate sin to suit the circumstances was failure to
keep God's Torah, His Law.

The modern apologist for traditional Judaism makes great play of the fact
that Torah does not mean law but instruction. While Ezra and his successors
would doubtless have agreed with the sentiment, it is not likely that they
would have accepted its implications. Scholars are apt to discuss how much
Judaism took over from the Persians and their religion, but they seldom mention their concept of law. When we compare Dan. 3 with Dan. 6, in the
former we find an oriental despot who decrees to satisfy his whim and changes
his mind more quickly than he had first decided. In the latter we find a ruler
bound by the sanctity of law, even though he had come to see its folly: the laws
of the Medes and Persians did not change, though they might be circumvented.

Ezra and his circle seem to have been profoundly impressed by this concept.
The Torah might be instruction, but it was not instruction a man might leave
behind him as his nation and its citizens grew up into a deeper knowledge of
God. Growth meant a challenge to apply not merely the principles of the
Torah but also its ordinances, commandments and statutes to cover ever
increasing areas of life. This was to be done logically and inexorably without

regard for the possible consequences. The time came later, when relaxations were made in order to preserve the life both of Israel and of individuals, but both then and down till today little thought has been given to the fate of the innocent who are made to suffer by man's misunderstanding of God's will, unless indeed Jewry as a whole or a major community is felt to be threatened.

It is impossible to know whether the action mentioned in Neh. 9:2 was, like that in 13:1–3, based on Deut. 23:3–5. Certainly vv. 7, 8 in their reference to Edom show that Moses was not intending a general separation from all outside Israel. It was so easy, however, to infer that if some were to be excluded then all should be, and it was much safer too.

Things were even worse where mixed marriages were concerned. That they were forbidden by the Torah is clear enough, cf. Exod. 34:16, Deut. 7:3, but there is nowhere any suggestion that they were not marriages, nor is there any punishment laid down for those that practise them. Ezra's logic was simple enough, and it has been repeated all too often by Christians, especially Roman Catholics. Because God condemned such marriages, it was inferred that they were not marriages at all. The men involved were put to public shame and presumably all had to bring a guilt offering, cf. Ezr. 10:19. But it was the women, who in most cases had no guilt, who had to bear the brunt of separation. They were turned loose with their children to go wherever they might, nor may we assume that they necessarily had their old homes to return to. There is no indication that Ezra was in the least concerned about the possible fate of the children thus turned loose on the world.

Here we see the beautiful simplicity of Ezra's concept. The keeping of the Torah did not merely mean the carrying out of what was expressly commanded in the Pentateuch. It did not even mean conforming to the interpretation which Ezra, with the power of the Persian state behind him, pronounced as official. It involved the applying of these principles to every conceivable aspect of life, even if they were unknown in the time of Moses.

Where these extensions were in conflict with age-old tradition they were bitterly opposed by many of the priests, who were, after all, guardians of tradition. Where they bore heavily on their lives and pockets, they met the passive resistance both of the land-owner and of the common people. But there is no evidence that Ezra's basic concept was ever seriously challenged. It needed the best part of a millennium before the imposing edifice of Jewry's religious law was finally worked out, and even then it had ceaselessly to be adapted to new circumstances as they arose, but it was all inherent in the principles which Ezra brought with him from Babylonia.

Ezra presumably returned soon after to the court of Artaxerxes; he disappears from the pages of history and not even Jewish tradition really knows anything more about him. But he left behind him his "judges and magistrates", who were doubtless paralleled in Babylonia and Persia, and they guaranteed that his work would continue.

We can best explain this silence by the intense hostility his reforms will have created in the Jerusalem priesthood and to a less degree among the city's richer families. The communication of the Torah to the common people and the laying of responsibility for its keeping on them automatically decreased the authority of the chief priests. Though this became clear to all only a couple of centuries later, the probability must have been clear even during Ezra's lifetime to the thoughtful. Ezra's principles placed the poorer citizen religiously on the same level as the noble and rich, so they too in many cases were hostile and sided with the priests.

Stress is often laid on the value of rabbinic tradition. In practice it seldom shows validity before 100 B.C. The carriers of tradition at an earlier date were the chief priestly families, who had no interest in keeping alive memories of a man they bitterly disliked. It is unprovable, but the probable dislocations in Ezra-Nehemiah, though not deliberate, may well reflect this dislike and lack of interest.

9

THE JEWS IN THE PERSIAN DISPERSION

In view of the very little information we have about Judea under Persian rule, it is entirely to be expected that we should know even less about those Jews that remained in Babylonia and surrounding districts or had found their way to other lands. Archaeology, which has thrown so much light on some other periods, has almost nothing to tell us here, though, as we saw in ch. 6, it has lifted the veil on a fascinating and completely unexpected Jewish community in Upper Egypt.

In Babylonia and the neighbouring countries it has revealed little more than that the Jewish Murashu family were able to set up as bankers on a considerable scale, and that the background of the book of Esther is accurate. It has nothing, however, to tell us that would throw more light on the story itself or the problems it raises. We cannot even identify the King Ahasuerus of the book of Esther with certainty. Usually he is taken to be Xerxes (486–465 B.C.), but there are a few front-rank archaeologists who prefer to think of Artaxerxes II (404–359 B.C.). The former gives us a satisfactory explanation of the time gap between Est. 1 : 3 and 2 : 16, for this would be the period when Xerxes was engaged in his disastrous campaign against Greece, which ended with the defeats at Salamis and Plataea. The latter removes the difficulties raised by Herodotus' mention of Xerxes' queen Amestris who cannot be identified with either Vashti or Esther, but does not explain the already mentioned time lapse. Since very little in the interpretation of the story depends on the identification of the monarch, he will simply be called by his Biblical name.

The evidence of archaeology is that the book gives an accurate background picture of the Persian court, a picture that could hardly have been obtainable by a story teller in the later Greek period. This has convinced most scholars that the late date once generally attributed to it cannot be defended. The best evidence that it is not the work of a pious inventor is given by the additions it received in the Greek translation, which may be found in the Apocrypha; these supply some of that religious element so obviously lacking in the Hebrew. The fact of these additions suggests, however, that the book was late in being taken into the canon. Though its canonicity seems not to have been discussed at the rabbinic council at Yavneh or Jamnia, there is adequate evidence that in later Talmudic times there were misgivings about certain aspects of the book. This may also explain why it, alone of all the canonical books, has not been found among the Qumran texts and fragments.

We do not know when the celebration of Purim began in Palestine. The New Testament does not mention it, at any rate by name, and there are few details in the earlier Talmudic writings—there are only about seven mentions of it in the Mishnah. Even Edersheim in his books about the Temple and Judaism in the time of Christ has few details to offer us. At the same time it was universally observed in the first century of our era. Josephus (*Ant.* XI, vi, 13) can say, "Whence it is, that even now all the Jews that are in the habitable earth keep these days festival". 2 Macc. 15 : 36 shows us that it was known in Egypt, and so indubitably in Palestine, by 50 B.C. We may perhaps deduce from its non-mention in the similar passage in 1 Macc. 7 : 49, which is normally dated some fifty years earlier, that the feast was not observed in Palestine at that time.

Mordecai and Esther

The story of Esther is throughout linked with Susa, or Shushan. This had been the capital of Elam; it was captured by the rising power of the Medo-Persian empire and became one of the three Persian royal cities, along with Ecbatana and Persepolis. Archaeology suggests that it was divided in two by the river Choaspes, the part on the left bank being the royal quarter, called in the Hebrew "the citadel"; this rendering is followed by Moffatt and JB. AV, RV "the palace" is too narrow, RSV, NEB "the capital" too wide, for in 3 : 15; 8 : 15 it seems to be distinguished from Susa the city. Possibly "royal quarter" would give the sense best. There was a considerable Jewish population in Susa, which was quite natural, as it was the nearest of the three Persian capitals to the area in which the Judean exiles had been settled.

There is no warrant for Josephus' claim that Mordecai was living in Babylon at the time when the story opens, and that he moved to Susa when Esther was taken into the royal harem. The statement that he "was sitting at the king's gate" (2 : 19, 21) can mean only that he was a court official, which is recognized explicitly by the apocryphal addition. The fact that he had to pass on his knowledge of the plot against the king's life through the queen (2 : 22) shows that his post was a relatively minor one.

We have every reason for thinking that Mordecai was a typical example of the aptitude shown by many Jews right down the long centuries of exile to make themselves at home in their alien surroundings, when they have been friendly. In private he was doubtless a practising Jew—if Ahasuerus was Xerxes, then Mordecai lived before Ezra and the increased demands of the Law introduced by him—but his antecedents were unknown among the multinational multitude that filled the minor court appointments. Since Zoroastrianism, the court religion, was not idolatrous and could be construed as monotheistic, there was no need for him to make a religious stand. His name Mordecai was doubtless derived from Marduk, the chief god of Babylon. Since it was from his father Jair that he received it (2 : 5), he was evidently brought up in a spirit of adaptation—we need not go so far as to call it assimilation. There is no need, as do so many sceptics, to make Kish in his genealogy (2 : 5) not his great-grandfather but King Saul's father, and so to suggest that the story states that Mordecai himself had been deported from Jerusalem, which would have made him well over a hundred years old. The names of Kish and Saul must have been treasured and frequently used in the tribe of Benjamin, witness the great apostle to the Gentiles, who at home and among his own people was known as Saul. Lest we are tempted to read too much into Mordecai's name, let us remember that it was borne also by one of the more important persons who returned with Zerubbabel (Ezr. 2:2).*

Whenever the Jew has been allowed free contacts with his surroundings, it has been fairly common for him to have two names, one Hebrew, one derived from his environment. We need look no further than "Saul, who is also called Paul". So Mordecai's niece Hadassah was known to her Gentile neighbours as Esther, which is derived from Ishtar, the most important of the Mesopotamian goddesses, the ruler of the planet Venus. Such a view is obviously displeasing to the average orthodox Jew, as may be seen in Rabbi M. Turetsky's suggesting that the name Esther may have been given her at her coronation (were Persian queens crowned?). The additional statement, "all scholars agree, however, that the name Esther is almost certainly derived from the Persian *stara*, star", might have been reasonably true half a century and more ago, but hardly today.†

We do not know who wrote this book. In default of further information Jewish tradition suggests Mordecai himself. The time, however, had not yet come when prime ministers wrote their memoirs. In addition, when Mordecai grew too old for his task or was supplanted by a new favourite, his downfall was probably as complete, though less dramatic, as Haman's. We shall probably be correct in assuming that he hired a professional writer to do the task. His touch may be seen in the element of exaggeration we constantly meet in everything to do with the Oriental ruler; perhaps it would be better to say that things are seen rather larger than life. If we remember this, we shall be able to see much in clearer perspective.

When we read the advice of Ahasuerus' courtiers, "Let the king appoint officers in all the provinces of his kingdom to gather all the beautiful young virgins to the harem in Susa the palace" (2:3), we need not take it any more literally than would the king. Quite apart from the fact that even a Xerxes would not have wantonly stirred up trouble throughout his empire, shaken by the disasters in Greece, by foolishly infringing the privacy of the women's quarters everywhere, he was not a sexual maniac. We are involved in enormity, if we imagine royal officers in the provinces from the Punjab to the first cataract on the Nile, and to Macedonia and the Caspian, picking out every girl of marriageable age who showed an exceptional degree of beauty and dispatching her to Susa. In addition, this was not an exercise to fill the royal harem but to find a new queen. Persian tradition was that the queen should be from a noble Iranian family. Ahasuerus might ignore the strict demands of tradition, but that does not mean that the new queen might be a lowly commoner picked up from the gutter, as the legend pictures King Cophetua doing with his beggar maid. There will, at the very least, have been a tacit understanding that

---

* An article by Rabbi Prof. L. L. Rabinowitz in *The Jerusalem Post* (7.3.74) agrees with the general position taken up above, but suggests that "sitting in the king's gate" (2:19, 21) meant that he was a judge in the supreme court. This is possible but hardly borne out by the detail in the story.

† In an article in *Jewish Chronicle* (London) of 8.3.74.

beauty was confined to the higher ranks of society.

Here we find the most probable explanation why Mordecai had told his niece not to reveal that she was a Jewess (2 : 10). That she was considered to be Mordecai's daughter the story presupposes, but it was not known at the time that he was a Jew. There is no vestige of evidence for any anti-Jewish sentiment at the Persian court, but for all that the Jews were a doubly subject race, conquered by the conquered Babylonians. With their Babylonian names uncle and niece were presumably taken to belong to some old Babylonian family.

Jewish sentiment was later shocked by the thought that Mordecai could have handed his adopted daughter over to a heathen marriage at best, or if the gamble did not come off, to an existence of opulent non-existence in a heathen harem (2 : 14). So tradition invented the idea that Mordecai had hidden her, but that he had been forced to bow to the king's command and hand her over.

The rabbis were also offended by the thought that the salvation of the Jews at that time depended to such an extent on the physical beauty of a young woman. Rabbi M. Turetsky, quoted above, states that there are five opinions in the classical Jewish sources about her age at the time. Four of them make her seventy or older. "She captivated all by an inner moral beauty of a magnetic type which attracted her beholders from king to eunuch." In fact she must have been thirteen or fourteen, and we should remember this when we think of her fears, her courage and her wisdom.

Haman the Agagite

Already Josephus (*Ant.* XI. vi. 5) gives us the haggadic interpretation, later found in the Targum, that Haman was a descendant of Agag, the Amalekite king (1 Sam. 15 : 8, 32, 33). So it is suggested that we have here, so to speak, the second round between one linked with Saul and a descendant of the last of the Amalekite kings. There is nothing to commend the idea.

The names Hammedatha (Haman's father), Haman, and those of Haman's ten sons (9 : 7–9) are all good Persian ones, and there is nothing in Agagite that is necessarily not Persian. No suggestion is made that Haman had any objection to the Jews as such; indeed, it is made clear, that if they were to share Mordecai's fate, it was merely to be to the greater glory of the king's favourite (3 : 6). Even more important is that the author does not leave overmuch to our imagination. Had he meant the haggadic interpretation he would have made it clear, which it is not. In the LXX translation Agagite appears as "the Bugaean". Whether or not we are to understand this as Braggart we cannot now say, but it does show that the later haggadic interpretation was not yet in circulation.

In essence there is nothing out of the ordinary in Haman's character and actions. He is one of the types thrown up by a dictatorship that makes no effort to hide its absolute power. He reminds me of Goering, who in many ways outshone his master Hitler and behaved as though he was the real power in the land. Yet, when it came to a crisis, he was crushed as easily as was Haman.

The position of grand vizier, if we may use a later term, under the Persian monarchs was one of immense power and of equally great danger. Ambitious men might close their minds to the fact that the same whim that raised them to power could and probably would cast them down in ruin. For all that they could not shut their unconscious minds to the threat, and the pressure of constant threat produced men like Haman.

No indication is given why Mordecai refused to prostrate himself before Haman; a court position implied prostration before the king and any on whom the king chose to bestow signal honour. Any suggestion must remain conjecture, but the reason may be suggested by "after these things" (3 : 1), with which the story of Haman begins. Though Mordecai's adopted daughter was queen and he had saved the king's life, no reward or advancement had come his way. Now he saw this worthless braggart promoted without reason or merit. It seems likely that he was suddenly overcome by a sense of the vanity and futility of his manner of life. This in turn awoke the realization that the only real value in his life was that he belonged to the people of God, as is shown by his open confession to his fellow-officials that he was a Jew (3 : 4).

When we read of the reaction of Haman's pride, we are confirmed in our belief that both Satan's and man's root sin was pride, the belief that one can control the issues of life and death not merely for oneself but also for others. Haman knew that it was a simple matter to crush Mordecai, cf. 5 : 11–14, and its very simplicity he felt as a personal insult.

It is quite characteristic of pride that it should be combined with a high degree of superstition (3 : 7). Pride does not bow to God, but it has an irrational fear of the blind forces of the universe; let the day but be propitious, and Haman was prepared to let the plan of revenge be known almost a year in advance. So confident was Haman that he discounted both the possibilities of flight and self-defence. The story-teller sums up the callousness of unbridled power, when he pictures Ahasuerus and Haman carousing, while even the predominantly Gentile Susa feels dismay (3 : 15).

The Collapse of the Plot

Mordecai was a proud man as well as Haman, and he too had to pay the price of pride; his pride as a Jew had been even more fatal than his place-seeking. In the skilful, objective account no mention is made of his religious reaction, but in fact there are no grounds for thinking that there was much disparity between his private reaction and his public expression of it. He was one of those successful men for whom religion is more a background than a daily reality. When disaster stared him in the face, there was no panic throwing of himself into religion. We can hear confidence in, "If you keep silence at such a time as this, relief and deliverance will rise for the Jews from another place" (4 : 14)—like many a politician today, who cannot get beyond Providence, Mordecai had forgotten how to talk about God—but it is confidence in the security of Israel, not of the individual. His attitude is largely, "God helps those who help themselves".

From the moment Queen Esther is prepared to sacrifice herself all the elements of the story begin to combine smoothly. Ahasuerus realized that his wife must have had a major request, if she was willing to risk her life for it; it had to be more than the pleasure of his presence at a banquet. The mention of Haman suggested to the king that he must be involved in the granting of the still unspoken request; in fact it was to prevent his becoming suspicious. While the postponement of the request (5 : 8) will have heightened the king's curiosity, it will hardly have been due to skilful stage-management on Esther's part. Rather the Holy Spirit caused a sudden spasm of fear, which gave Him added time to work, so that when Haman's star was eclipsed, Mordecai's was able to shine out in full splendour.

With the fall and death of Haman the peril for the Jews had passed, but Esther, doubtless on Mordecai's advice, decided to make doubly sure. The decree, thanks to the Persians' stress on the immutability of the king's commands, could not be revoked, but it could be effectively neutralized. When the people of the Queen and Grand Vizier were allowed to defend themselves (8 : 11), we may be sure that the authorities knew very well on which side their bread was buttered.

The effect was immediate. "Many . . . declared themselves Jews" (8 : 17)—the RV rendering "became Jews" does not do justice to the Hebrew—though their adherence probably lasted in most cases for just as long as Mordecai was Grand Vizier. In addition, when the day of reckoning came, there were eight hundred victims of Jewish revenge in Susa, including Haman's ten sons; there were seventy-five thousand elsewhere in the Persian empire.

Our distaste, to put it no more strongly, for such a bloody revenge normally keeps us from examining the figures more closely. Eight hundred in Susa was a high figure for a city where there was no very big Jewish population. In proportion, the other figure is low and could easily represent Jewish vengeance in the province of Babylon alone.

One of the reasons why the truth of this book has been so widely questioned by scholars is that, apart from the Feast of Purim, its events seem to have left no mark on records anywhere. When the leaders of the Jewish community at Yeb, cf. p. 23, wrote to the high priest in Jerusalem and later to Bagoas, the Persian governor of Judea, and the two sons of Sanballat, they did not mention in their summary of events that it was not so long that the very existence of the community had been threatened. Equally, in the enumeration of opposition in Ezr. 4 : 6–23, Haman's decree is not even hinted at. All the trouble begins with the Jews' neighbours, who try to influence the Persian court. We can only infer that Haman's decree was never promulgated in the satrapies Beyond-the-River and Egypt. A satrap had almost boundless power, and he would have to decide how to handle something obviously expressing the king's passing whim. In some satrapies there were no Jews. In others, like Beyond-the-River, an attempt to carry out the decree could well have resulted in a general explosion, so probably both the original order and then the permission for the Jews to defend themselves quietly vanished without trace in the provincial archives.

This would explain why the feast of Purim and the book of Esther seem to be relatively late arrivals on the Palestinian scene. If this is so, the only real argument against the historicity of the story seems to disappear.

Without a Jewish queen and grand vizier there might well have never been a

Nehemiah and Ezra, but it is the latter who are of real importance for the history of the Jews and the development of Judaism.

The Book of Tobit

The Book of Tobit is a charming piece of fiction comparatively well known because of its place in the Apocrypha. It claims to describe some of the experiences of Tobit, a pious member of the tribe of Naphtali, who had been deported by the Assyrians, and of his son Tobias. Though its fictional nature has been long recognized, except by some Roman Catholic scholars, it has been valued for the picture it gives of the ideals of the pious in the Eastern dispersion. Though with the exception of some Aramaic MSS it was preserved only in Greek—the Latin and Syriac are translations from the Greek—it was generally accepted that behind it lay a Hebrew original. Parts of this have now been found at Qumran.

Formerly, on internal evidence, most scholars had dated it about 200 B.C. In 1966, however, Albright was able to state with confidence, on the strength of the Hebrew used in the fragments discovered at Qumran, "We can date such books as Esther and Tobit in the late Persian period . . ."*

This means we can gain some impression of the religious life of the pious in the East at the time. Though Tobit's heart obviously goes out to the temple in Jerusalem, there is no suggestion of an attempt to attend its services. Obviously the pilgrimages, which were such a feature of a later age, had not yet begun. There is also no suggestion of the existence of the Synagogue, which is all too often taken for granted as a product of the exile from the first.

Tobit takes the authority of the Torah and of the Prophets for granted; there are considerable echoes of the Psalms, Proverbs and Job. There are also indications of a growing oral tradition. Prayer in time of need recurs whenever it is needed, but there is no suggestion of regular daily prayer. Charity to the needy and sexual purity are stressed. All this adds up to a picture of rudimentary Judaism, and it probably shows the kind of influence that Ezra's reform made on the pious, especially those separated from the Temple and its ritual.

* D. N. Freedman & J. C. Greenfield (editors), *New Directions in Biblical Archaeology* (Doubleday), p. 15.

10
JUDEA IN THE LATE
PERSIAN PERIOD

We know virtually nothing of the approximately hundred years that elapsed in Judea between the work of Ezra and Nehemiah and the coming of the Greeks. Were it not for the long drawn-out struggle between the Greeks and Persians at this time and the fascinated curiosity of Greeks who visited the court of the Great King, we should know virtually nothing of Persia's wider history also. So our ignorance of what took place in Judea is not surprising.

Josephus tells us (*Ant.* XI. vii. 1) that in the time of Bagoas, a Persian governor after Nehemiah, known to us also from the papyri from Elephantine, the high-priest John killed his brother Jeshua in the temple-precincts. As a penalty Bagoas both entered the Temple and for seven years imposed a tax of fifty shekels for each lamb offered in the public sacrifices. If Josephus is correct in saying that Jeshua was a friend of Bagoas and was intriguing to obtain the high-priesthood, his brother's action becomes more understandable, though in default of further information we may not condone it. The strange thing is that Bagoas does not seem to have inflicted any real punishment on the culprit, for the tax hit the people as a whole. Oesterley is probably correct in suggesting that the very heavy fine—a minimum of two lambs was offered each day as a public offering (Num. 28 : 3)—was a punishment for rebellious dissatisfaction among the people.*

Some twenty years before Alexander the Great shattered the Persian empire a very serious revolt broke out in Phoenicia, which took three years to quell. There are a few indications that Judea was also affected, but the extremer deductions by some scholars of large-scale deportation to the south of the Caspian Sea had better be taken with a large pinch of salt. M. Noth and J. Bright in their histories of Israel show their wisdom by ignoring the whole question. Probably the main reason why these slight indications have been welcomed by some is that this alleged calamity allows them a place for psalms which extremer critics had earlier attributed to the Maccabean period, but which they do not want to move back to the time of the monarchy. Had the calamity justified the language of the psalms in question, it is incredible that it would have left as good as no trace on Jewish memory.

The Samaritan Schism

Even though we cannot fill in the details with certainty, one thing of the greatest historical importance happened in this period, viz. the religious break between the Samaritans and Jerusalem, which we call the Samaritan schism.

* Oesterley and Robinson, *A History of Israel*, Vol. II, p. 140.

If the relationship between the Persian sub-provinces of Samaria and Judea had remained on the level of political hostility, based mainly on meaningless memories of the past that had irrevocably vanished, it is likely that it would gradually have become normal. When placed within the larger context of the satrapy Beyond-the-River, and especially in the framework of the Persian Empire, large even by modern standards, the old rivalry had as much real meaning as the annual international Rugby clashes on the sports field. Unfortunately a religious element was added to it, and the bitterness engendered has remained to the present day, though at last it seems to be vanishing among the five hundred or fewer survivors of the Samaritans.

The dominant view both in Jewish and Christian circles that passages like Deut. 12:5–7, 11–14; 16:2; 26:2 demand one exclusive central sanctuary is probably incorrect.* A comparison of Deut. 12:14 and 23:16 (Heb. 23:17) will show that the language used need not be given a purely exclusive interpretation. Josiah's action in leaving Jerusalem as the only operative shrine may just as well have been motivated by his feeling that only so could he finally stamp out idolatry and corrupt religion. It is far more likely that though there was a central sanctuary at which the Ark of the Covenant was lodged, there were a limited number of other lawful sanctuaries, which had been marked out by Divine appearances or theophanies. In addition there were the many illegitimate "high places". Though we know of no such theophany at Shiloh or Gibeon, we need not doubt that there had been one. It should be noted that while there was doubtless a sanctuary at Samaria itself, in the absence of any well-authenticated theophany it was never able to displace Bethel as the leading shrine of the Northern kingdom.

It was not the building, or even the ritual furniture, at a sanctuary that made the place holy, but the appearance of God or of the angel of the Lord (Jdg. 6:11, 2 Sam. 24:16–18) had left a virtually indelible quality of holiness there—natural phenomena would normally account for the choice of "high places". This holiness persisted whether or not men continued to worship there, so the Israelites after the conquest of Canaan could restart their worship in the places where the Patriarchs had left off centuries before. This holiness was not affected by the destruction of buildings and altar, cf. 1 Ki. 18:30. The story of Josiah at Bethel and the other sanctuaries of Samaria (2 Ki. 23:15–20) shows how a holy place could be profaned, i.e. made common ground once more.

Josiah acted similarly with the high places of Judah (2 Ki. 23:8, 10, 13), which in practice doubtless included the sanctuaries at Hebron and Beersheba, where there had in fact been theophanies. It may be that Shiloh's complete lapse into obscurity, once the Philistines had destroyed it, was due to their carrying out some similar ceremony to destroy the holiness of the site that was the visible centre of Israel's unity.

The heathen settlers in Samaria accepted the Mosaic law (2 Ki. 17:24–34), but quite naturally followed the religious customs of the remnants of the northern tribes—no later date for their acceptance of the Law really makes

* Cf. especially Brinker, *The Influence of Sanctuaries in Early Israel*, pp. 199f.

sense, least of all one after Ezra. This made their assimilation with the old population the more rapid, and their heathen cults, separated from the soil in which they had grown up, gradually withered away. Josiah's great reforming drive through Samaria, mentioned earlier, deprived this mixed people of any places of worship for which they could claim any degree of holiness.

We need not doubt that in the description of Josiah's passover (2 Chr. 35:1–19) the Israelites mentioned as being present were not exceptions, but that a good section of those who took part had come from Samaria. Similarly we find pilgrims from Shechem, Samaria and Shiloh coming to the ruins of the Jerusalem temple after it had been destroyed (Jer. 41:45)—there is nowhere any suggestion that the Babylonians had deliberately profaned it. Doubtless such pilgrimages continued throughout the period of the exile, for, as already said, the holiness of the site did not depend on the buildings.

In spite of sentimental exaggeration by some modern writers, there is no suggestion that the Samaritans were ever excluded from the Temple site. The refusal (Ezr. 4:3) was to let them join in the building operations, presumably because it would have given them certain prescriptive rights in it. There is no evidence that the exclusion from Israel of those of foreign origin (Neh. 13:3) included Samaritans, nor are they listed among the foreign wives (Neh. 13:23, Ezr. 9:1). In a population that had become predominantly Israelite, it would have become impossible to isolate the foreign elements, even though it was felt an insult for a priest to marry a woman of such questionable descent (Neh. 13:28).

We know from Josephus that they were not excluded from the Temple until the time of Christ, and then it was only because they had tried to desecrate it with corpses (*Ant.* XVIII.ii.2). For the Talmudic rabbis they were *minim* (heretics or schismatics), who would have been welcomed at any time, if they had abjured their peculiar views. If things are different today, it is merely because of the outworking of rabbinic marriage laws, which makes it almost impossible for the Bne Yisrael from India, Falashas from Abyssinia, Karaites, and even more Samaritans to be welcomed into the orthodox Jewish fold, although their status as Jews is recognized.

It must have been most galling, therefore, for the Samaritans in the time of tension that reached its climax under Nehemiah to have to use the Jerusalem temple, or alternatively one to which the quality of holiness could not legitimately be ascribed.

The Temple on Mt. Gerizim

We are told by Nehemiah, that he drove out a grand-son of Eliashib, the high-priest, when he first came to Jerusalem (3:1), because he had married one of Sanballat's daughters (13:28). Josephus, on the other hand, tells us (*Ant.* XI.vii.2; viii.2) that Eliashib's great-grandson Manasseh, brother of Jaddua the high-priest, an older contemporary of Alexander the Great, was married to the daughter of a Sanballat, who had been made governor of Samaria by Darius III, the last king of Persia. The people insisted on his divorcing his Samaritan wife, so he went to Sanballat, who promised to build him a temple on Mt. Gerizim. The promise was fulfilled by permission of Alexander the Great, whose side Sanballat and the Samaritans had taken (*Ant.* XI. viii. 4). According to Josephus, Manasseh was joined by a number of priests and Levites who were in similar matrimonial difficulties. Later others came as well, who had fallen foul of the religious authorities in Jerusalem. Doubtless they were mainly those who did not approve of Ezra's interpretation of the Law, rather than, as Josephus half suggests, bad characters.

Because Josephus' account is tied up with the story of the respect and awe with which Alexander treated Jaddua, the high-priest, a story which today is almost universally regarded as an edifying piece of pro-Jewish invention, and also because he knew so little of the Persian period, and what he did was often inaccurate, until recently it has been generally assumed that he had erred here too. So it is claimed that Josephus is giving no more than a blown up version of Nehemiah's expulsion of Eliashib's unnamed grandson. We may, however, give him the benefit of the doubt.

Josephus had no motive for separating the schism from Nehemiah's time, the more so as he admired him. We know from other sources that there were two and possibly three Sanballats, presumably all of the same family, who were governors of Samaria. Many scholars have on general principles agreed that the building of the Gerizim temple would have been more likely under the Greeks than the Persians. Nor may we forget that Josephus, a priest himself, indubitably had access as a younger man to priestly records and traditions. Finally, the situation as depicted by him, where there was popular support for strictness in the application of the Law with a priestly and Levitical group, possibly appealing to older traditions, opposed to it, would suit a somewhat later period better than that of Nehemiah himself.

However that may be, a temple was duly built on Mt. Gerizim. The reason for the choice is not hard to find. It is the only site mentioned by name in the Torah for the worship of God after the conquest (Deut. 11:29; 27:4–8, 11–14). The Samaritan Pentateuch, followed by the Old Latin, reads Mt. Gerizim in 27:4 instead of Mt. Ebal, cf. NEB mg; Josh. 8:30 has Mt. Ebal. At this distance of time it is impossible to know with certainty whether the obviously deliberate alteration was made by Samaritan or Judean scribes.*

As recent discoveries at Wadi Daliyeh confirm,† Alexander had Samaria destroyed, many of its leading citizens put to death, and a new city built peopled mainly by his veteran soldiers. The Samaritans rebuilt Shechem, so bringing their chief town and sanctuary together.

Their priesthood was a Zadokite one, and they had brought with them the old priestly traditions from Jerusalem, traditions which were in some respects stricter than those enforced by Ezra and his successors. Real bitterness between the two sides probably showed itself first in the time of the Hasmonean priest-king John Hyrcanus (134–104 B.C.). He captured the whole of Samaria and

---

* According to Rabbinic tradition there are as many as eighteen passages, where they claim they had changed the text for to them adequate reasons.

† F. M. Cross, *Papyri of the Fourth Century B.C. from Daliyeh* in D. N. Freedman & J. C. Greenfield (editors), *New Directions in Biblical Archaeology*.

destroyed the temple on Mt. Gerizim (107 B.C.).* This was not simply an act of spite. Even as he had earlier forced the Idumeans to accept Judaism, so now he was forcing the Samaritans to conform to Jerusalem's version of Judaism. When the Samaritans were freed from Jewish rule by the coming of the Romans, there remained a legacy of bitterness that could not be bridged. So while in one sense the Samaritan schism began with the return of the Jews from exile, in another it was made unhealable by the action of John Hyrcanus.

For the Jews it was not the Temple as such that mattered. There is no evidence that they felt very strongly about the strange sanctuary at Elephantine, or the later copy of the Jerusalem temple at Leontopolis in Egypt. What mattered was the Samaritans' proud, defiant claim that this was the holy place chosen by God (Jn. 4 : 20), that they had an Aaronic priesthood superior to the Hasmoneans, who took over the office in Jerusalem in the middle of the second century, and that they interpreted the Law according to an older tradition—so they claimed—than that in force in Jerusalem. In many points it seems to have been stricter than that of the Pharisees, as was indeed also that of the Sadducees.

This meant spiritual warfare in which there could be no compromise. Later the Christian was to face the rabbinic Jew with a clear-cut either-or, but the Samaritans threatened to undermine the authority of the rabbinic leaders, while in large measure appearing to agree with them. The attitude of many a hyper-orthodox rabbi to the Liberal and Reform leaders today doubtless mirrors the way in which his ancestors looked on those of the Samaritans.

Religion in the Late Persian Period

Carlyle quotes an unnamed and unidentified philosopher as saying, "Happy the people whose annals are vacant", and this is in many ways the judgment to be passed on Judea in the Persian period. For perhaps the only time in their history the Jews were able to stand aside from world-history, their troubles belonging more to the parish pump than to the destiny of nations. Even the Fertile Crescent seemed largely to have sunk into slumber waiting for the coming of the West, led by the he-goat of Dan. 8 : 5, i.e. Alexander the Great. That is perhaps why Dan. 11 : 2 enumerates only four kings of Persia, where the modern historian knows of at least eleven.

In such a setting, once Zerubbabel had passed from the scene, and with him the hopes of the Davidic dynasty, the high-priest became inevitably the natural representative of the people, the more so as it was to religion that the Persians granted autonomy. So began that unique feature of Jewish history in which most of its real leaders were also leading figures in its religion. Political power often corrupted the religious leaders, but it meant that political power normally remained a means to an end, not an end in itself. In addition, while Jewry's leaders, when the people were prospering, were normally rich, sometimes very rich, riches were also regarded as a means to a better end.

In Babylonia and Persia concepts from Zoroastrianism gradually seeped into

---

* After Bar Cochba's revolt (A.D. 132–135), as an extra punishment on the Jews, the Romans allowed the Samaritans to rebuild the Gerizim temple. This was destroyed by the now dominant Christian Church in 484. The mountain top is still regarded as holy by the Samaritans, who have their Passover sacrifice there.

Jewish consciousness, but on their way to Judea they lost much of their force and never played much part in standard Judaism. We find them in the New Testament, but in such an attenuated form that they merely enrich the heights and depths of Christian theology.

As a result the hard-working farmers of Judea had little theology to distract them as they tried to assimilate the lessons of the exile and the implications of Ezra's presentation of the Law. The absurdities of pilpul* and casuistic hair-splitting in East European town ghettos and village *shtetls* or in the narrow alleys of Mea Shearim tend to hide from us that for much of its history rabbinic legalism was extraordinarily down to earth and in touch with reality. It is insufficiently realized that well before the heroic times of the Maccabean brothers the life of the average Jew was strictly governed by the Law of Moses. The detailed application of it to every feature of life still lay in the future, but the firm foundations had been laid. We may attribute the greatness of this victory largely to the relatively unbroken calm of the later Persian period.

---

* Pilpul is the type of hair-splitting, logic-chopping argument to which the mediaeval schoolmen were also addicted.

11

THE COMING OF THE GREEKS

Persia's defeats at Marathon (490), Salamis (480), and Plataia (479), though humiliating, could be explained away as the result of fighting at the end of over-extended lines of communication. Even the victors continued to look on the ruler of Persia as the Great King, and warring factions vied for his favour. It was not until about 400 that discerning men began to realize how essentially weak the vast empire was. Cyrus, a prince of the royal blood and satrap of Asia Minor, wanted to wrest the throne from his brother, Artaxerxes II. He strengthened the forces available to him by hiring ten thousand Greek mercenaries. In a battle near Babylon Cyrus fell, but the Greeks had shown such valour, that even after their commanders had been tricked and killed they were allowed to withdraw. After major hazards they reached the shores of the Black Sea, and finally six thousand of them were able to return to Greece.* Ambitious men realized that Persia would not be able to stand against any well-organized and disciplined assault.

Internal disunity among the Greeks gave Persia another lease of life, but finally Alexander the Great, the "he-goat from the west" (Dan. 8:5), launched his invasion in 334. By 331 the Persian empire had ceased to exist and before Alexander died in 323 he was the undisputed master of a larger empire than one man had ever ruled over before.

It is not likely that Alexander's meteoric career had immediate effect on the Jews. His victory at Issus (333) meant that only Tyre and Gaza along the Mediterranean littoral resisted him. While Tyre had been able to resist Nebuchadnezzar for thirteen years, it held out against Alexander for only seven months. We may take it for granted that all the smaller cities of the Western Fertile Crescent hastened to make their peace with the victor. If there is any truth at all in Josephus' fanciful story of Alexander's meeting with the high priest, Jaddua (*Ant.* XI. viii. 4, 5), it will be that the conqueror treated the Jewish leader, who had come to yield up the city, with the same courtesy that he used as a matter of policy to all the oriental leaders who did not oppose him.

After Alexander's death his empire fell to pieces, and soon there were four clearly recognizable portions (Dan. 8:8), soon to be reduced to three. Only two were of importance to the Jews. Ptolemy, Alexander's personal staff-officer, had realized the strategic position of Egypt. He became its satrap and in due course its king; he made Alexandria, which had been founded by Alexander the Great, his capital. While the other leading generals were tearing themselves to bits, he followed the age-old strategy of the Pharaohs and quietly

* Xenophon, one of their two leaders, has given us the story in the *Anabasis*.

68

annexed Palestine and Coele-Syria to act as a shield for his desert frontier; later he was able to add the Phoenician coast. Seleucus, after fluctuations of fortune, emerged as ruler of most of Alexander's Asiatic possessions, with his capitals at Seleucia on the Tigris and Antioch on the Orontes.

The Political Consequences for the Jews

Josephus quotes a Greek writer Agatharchides* (*Contra Ap.* 1, 22, *Ant.* XII. i. 1), who mockingly told how Ptolemy had been able to capture Jerusalem by taking advantage of the Sabbath, when the Jews refused to take up arms. We need not doubt the truth of the story, but he was probably only making assurance doubly sure, for it is most doubtful whether the city would have resisted in any case. Both Josephus and the apocryphal *Letter of Aristeas* tell how Ptolemy deported a large number of Jews to Egypt, the majority of whom were apparently settled in Alexandria. They were not full citizens—for that they would have had to be founder members of the city—but they were given special privileges, which proved so attractive that they were soon joined voluntarily by others. This was the beginning of the Western diaspora or dispersion, which was to play such a tremendous part in Jewish history and also in the spread of the early Church.

Almost from the first there was cold war with frequent intervals of fighting between the Ptolemies and the Seleucids. This meant that for more than a century, until Antiochus III conquered Palestine in 198, there was a frontier between Judea and the large community of the Eastern diaspora in Mesopotamia and Persia. We have no information as to whether this hindered pilgrimages to Jerusalem, when there was no actual fighting, but it must have decreased the influence of the Eastern diaspora at a time when far-reaching influences were beginning their work in Judea. At all times the eastern diaspora exercised a conservative influence, and this political separation must have greatly helped forward the new Greek influences.

Under the Persians Judea had been a backwater. Normally trade between the East and Egypt avoided the desert and went by ship from the Phoenician ports to the Nile delta. Both under the Ptolemies and later under the Seleucids Palestine became a frontier province with all that this implied, including the constant movement of troops, and for practical reasons most of the commerce between the rival states will have passed through it.

This foreign influence was greatly enhanced by the planting of Greek settlements in Palestine. Already Alexander had settled some of his veterans in Samaria after a revolt by the Samaritans. Later Greek cities included Raphia, Gaza, Ascalon, Azotus (Ashdod), the Decapolis, Ptolemais (Acre), and at a later date Caesarea, Caesarea Philippi and Sepphoris, the capital of Galilee. In such a connection "Greek" does not necessarily mean Greek by race, but that Greek speech, customs, religion and municipal order had been accepted. The influence on the Jews was profound and as early as about 300 the Greek writer Hecataeus of Abdera could say, "The Jews have greatly modified the traditions of their fathers".

* 2nd. cent. B.C., known only by quotations from his works.

Hellenistic Civilization

The Greeks were convinced that they alone were the only truly civilized people, even though a historian like Herodotus (484–424) looked with admiration on what Egypt and Babylon had been able to achieve. Hence Alexander considered that he came as a benefactor to the lands he conquered, and this outlook remained a fixed belief among his successors. There was in addition the realization that only by a common culture and religion could they hope to bind together such varied peoples and cultures.

No culture can be transplanted without being changed, and this was true also of that of Greece, when it was brought to the peoples of the Eastern Mediterranean and Western Asia. The dialectal and cultural variations that had persisted in Greece itself were rapidly ironed out. Then when Egyptians, Syrians, Mesopotamians and Persians accepted what Greece had to offer them, something was bound to be lost. Scholars make the useful distinction by calling the original Greek product Hellenic, and the later and wider developments Hellenistic.

The centre of cultured Greek life had always been the city, the *polis*. The Hellenistic rulers never tried to impose a mass Greek civilization on their subjects; they could not have, even had they wanted to. They relied on their cities gradually to extend their civilizing influence over the countryside around. As the life of the *polis* had developed, it was essentially one for the cultured gentleman who had slaves to enable him to have sufficient leisure to give himself to polite pursuits. So we have to picture Hellenism as spreading from the city to the village, from the rich to the poor. The fact that most of the Jews in Judea were probably farmers with few slaves to give them leisure helps to explain why the majority were slow to be influenced by the new outlook on life.

There were two other factors that slowed up this influence. For Hellenism culture, language and religion were of importance, seldom physical descent, but as had been so strongly stressed in Ezra's time (Ezr. 9:2) the Jews were "the holy race". Then also Greek religion was, with minor exceptions, the worship of natural forces. Hence it was very easy to identify the Greek gods and goddesses with the equivalent nature deities, wherever Hellenism spread. If we compare the many-breasted image of Artemis (Diana) of the Ephesians, reproduced in so many Bible dictionaries and Biblical helps, with the beautiful huntress of Greek art, we shall gain some idea of what such syncretism, as it is called, meant. But an identifying of Jehovah with any of the gods of Olympus, though occasionally attempted in fringe sects, was inescapably apostasy. Monotheism, unless it remained a philosophical theory, was an abomination and folly to Hellenism.

Some indications of how limited the influence of Hellenism was outside the Greek cities are Syriac, i.e. Eastern Aramaic, translations of the Gospels, in spite of the influence of Antioch, Seleucia and other great cities, and Coptic ones in Egypt, in spite of the great Greek city of Alexandria, where the Septuagint, the Greek translation of the Old Testament was made. We may also think of the continued use of Lycaonian among the citizens of Lystra (Acts 14:11) and of their Punic dialect by the people of Malta (Acts 28 : 2), called for that reason "barbarians" by Luke.* Once we grasp this, we can more easily grasp the influence exerted by Hellenism. It can be compared with the Renaissance in the 15th and 16th centuries, or with the upsurge of the natural sciences last century; at first these movements influenced an elite, but then penetrated ever more widely into the general consciousness.

The orthodoxy of the Naturei Karta in the Mea Shearim quarter of Jerusalem seems even to most Jews to be an almost incredible fossil from antediluvian times. Yet there was a time when the attitude to life it reveals was almost universal among men, who were under the rule of religious law and superstition, which embraced most of the conceivable acts of life. We seldom realize to what extent even the greatest kings were caught up in a round of priest-led ceremonial and tabu. It was Greek thought, spread by Hellenism, that to a very great extent made man an autonomous being, just as it was the rediscovery of ancient Greece at the Renaissance that gave birth to modern humanism.

It may be doubted whether the ordinary Greek really realized what he was doing. The Greek games had started as a religious ceremony, and to the last they were held in honour of certain deities, but they soon led to the regarding of human physical achievements and human beauty as something good in themselves. The Greek theatre, both on its comic and tragic sides, had been part of religious worship. When, however, Athenian drama was at its height, man could both complain of and criticize the gods or laugh at them, so long as it was done on the stage. Finally, the philosopher was allowed to question anything and everything, provided that, at least in the earlier stages, he made clear that he was speaking of what could be and not of what was. The effect of all this was to make first the typical urban Greek and then those who drank deeply of the cup of Hellenism essentially individualists. It is no chance that Paul's missionary work should have been based on cities, normally of importance, and that the response to his preaching was mainly one of individuals.

It was not only the hard life of the farmer, dependent on his own and his family's labour, rather than that of the slave, that erected a dyke that protected the Jews of Judea from the incoming tide of Hellenism. Even where they were most exposed to it in cities like Alexandria and Antioch on the Orontes, the fact that its main public expression in the theatre, the stadium and the philosophers' schools was still officially, even if nominally, linked with the old pagan religion, made it impossible for the Jew who cared at all for the traditions of his ancestors to take any part or even be a silent spectator.

Jesus Ben Sira

The author of the apocryphal book commonly called Ecclesiasticus will perhaps serve best to illustrate the earlier stages of Hellenism's influence on the Jews. Jesus ben Sira was born some time after 250 in Jerusalem, while it was still under Ptolemaic rule, and he probably lived to see the Seleucids take over the lordship of Palestine.

* Though "barbarian" sometimes had similar connotations to the Greek speaker as to the English, it really meant one who did not speak Greek.

He was a scribe. The force of such a term is often misunderstood. Bentzen wrote, "The wise denotes not only philosophers. It may justly be said that the word signifies the educated class. It is characteristic that its members were people who knew the art of writing. Often they are called the scribes, but then generally a narrower circle is meant . . . functionaries of state. The scribes then are mediators of an international culture in the same manner as modern academicians".* Similarly Rylaarsdam stated, "The role of the sages and the public estimate of them were very similar in all lands. They were the schoolmasters and court counselors".† That is why in Sir. 38:24, where RSV translates literally "scribe", NEB rightly prefers "scholar", cf. also p. 41.

Ben Sira's estimate of the scholar is fascinating. He has a word of appreciation for the farmer (38:25, 26), the craftsman, smith and potter (38:27–30), for he knows that they are essential; "Without them a city would have no inhabitants; no settlers or travellers would come to it . . . they maintain the fabric of this world, and their daily work is their prayer" (38:32, 34). But he grows lyrical, when he comes to the scholar. "How different it is with the man who devotes himself to studying the law of the Most High, who investigates all the wisdom of the past, and spends his time studying the prophecies! . . . The great avail themselves of his services, and he is seen in the presence of rulers. He travels in foreign countries and learns at first hand the good or evil of man's lot. . . . The memory of him will not die but will live on from generation to generation" (39:1, 4, 9).

Though he gives us few details, it is clear that at one time he travelled fairly extensively (34:11, 12; 51:13), and it may be that his bitter picture of the plight of the stranger (29:21–28) is based on his experiences at this time. What official tasks he may have been engaged in we are not told, but in 51:5, 6 he thanks God for his deliverance "from the foul tongue and its lies—a wicked slander spoken in the king's presence. I came near to death; I was on the brink of the grave." At the time when he wrote his book he had a school, which he did not hesitate to recommend in the closing section of his book (51:23–30). One of the marked features is his denunciation of women, which clearly mirrors his own unhappy experiences in his family life, both with his wife and daughters.

One has only to compare Ben Sira with Proverbs, or even Qohelet (Ecclesiastes), to realize the tremendous difference between them. In the two earlier books authorship is relatively unimportant; as in all the Biblical writings the authors' personalities have left their mark, but we do not attempt the fruitless task of trying to recreate the writer from the evidence of his work. Even in the Davidic psalms the personal experience behind them has been so generalized that in many cases it cannot be recovered. But though Ben Sira seems to have thought that he was writing Scripture, cf. 24:33; 33:16–18, yet apparently he was unaware that, unlike his predecessors, he was essentially preaching himself. In other words he was an individualist in a way recognized neither by the Old nor the New Testament. Though Paul has much to say about himself in his

---

* *Introduction to the Old Testament*, I, pp. 170f.

† *Revelation in Jewish Wisdom Literature*, p. 9.

letters, it is in essence self-depreciatory. Ben Sira was not a proud man, but he was essentially self-complacent. This is a quality, it is worth adding, which we repeatedly find in later generations among the rabbis.

R. H. Pfeiffer put it very well, when he said, "Thus Sirach marks the transition from the Bible to the Talmud, from the authority of inspiration . . . to the authority of learning."* It is very doubtful whether he ever realized it, for he was a declared foe of Hellenism, but he had learnt his outlook from the philosophers whom he had met.

Because the time came when his book was blacklisted (c. A.D. 200), there are modern scholars who think that he was a Sadducee. The arguments for this are very tenuous, and it is far more likely that he was rejected for the same reason that the Tannaim—the rabbis between approximately the beginning of the Christian era and A.D. 250—got rid of all the extra-canonical books at this time. In their enforcement of their own views no voices might be heard other than the Scriptures themselves and their official interpretations of them. As we shall see in the next chapter Ben Sira antedated both Sadducees and Pharisees. Had he lived to see them, he would almost certainly have favoured the latter, but he would have felt superior to both parties.

Ben Sira then is the explanation of one of the most striking features in Rabbinic Judaism. While Scripture, especially the Torah, is treated with the greatest respect as God's revelation, yet it is handed over completely to the interpretation of the scholar. The classical expression of this is, of course, the story of R. Eliezer and his opponents. "On a certain occasion R. Eliezer (c. A.D. 100) used all possible arguments to substantiate his opinion, but the Rabbis did not accept it. He said, 'If I am right, may this carob tree move a hundred yards from its place.' it did so . . . They said, 'From a tree no proof can be brought.' Then he said, 'May the canal prove it.' The water of the canal flowed backwards. They said, 'Water cannot prove anything.' Then he said, 'May the walls of this House of Study prove it.' Then the walls of the house bent inwards, as if they were about to fall. R. Joshua rebuked the walls, and said to them, 'If the learned dispute about the Halakah (the rules of behaviour), what has that to do with you?' So to honour R. Joshua, the walls did not fall down, but to honour R. Eliezer, they did not quite straighten again. Then R. Eliezer said, 'If I am right, let the heavens prove it.' Then a *bat qol* (a voice from heaven) said, 'What have you against R. Eliezer? The Halakah is always with him.' Then R. Joshua got up and said, 'It is not in heaven' (Deut. 30 : 12). What did he mean by this? R. Jeremiah said, 'The Law was given us from Sinai. We pay no attention to a heavenly voice. For already from Sinai the Law said, By a majority you are to decide (Exod. 23 : 2).'"† This means quite simply that the rabbis believed that God had so delivered Himself into the hands of men by the revelation of the Torah, that it was for them to decide how He was to be served, provided that the decision was consistent with the Torah, or could be made to appear so.

We must go further. Sometimes—rarely maybe, but definitely for all that,

* *History of New Testament Times*, p. 369.

† *Bab.M.* 59b, quoted in C. G. Montefiore & H. Loewe, *A Rabbinic Anthology*, pp. 340f.

as in the case of Hillel's famous *prosbul**—they were prepared to set aside the plain teaching of the Torah. They might shrink back from Ben Sira as too great an individualist, laying too much stress on his own authority, but they entirely approved of his implicit acceptance of the authority of human reason and study, and this had come straight from Hellenism at its best. We shall see how the intolerance of Hellenism at its worst was to make Judaism turn its back on it decisively, but this legacy from the defeated foe was to remain down to the present day.

---

* Deut. 15 : 2 ordered the remitting of loans in the Sabbatical year. As a result it became increasingly diffi-cult to borrow as the Sabbatical year drew near. Hillel (1st cent. B.C.) introduced a scheme by which the creditor affirmed before a court of law that the collection of the debt was handed over to the court. Since public debts in contrast to private ones were not affected by the Sabbatical year, it was a guarantee of repay-ment and so made loans easier to obtain.

12
HELLENISM COMES TO JERUSALEM

The first clear revelation of what Hellenism could mean in practice came to Jerusalem through the challenge of the family of Tobias to the high priests, or rather to their political power. Historians, taking advantage of the fact that there were three high priests in this period called Onias (in Hebrew Choni), refer to the rival parties as Oniads and Tobiads.*

Since like appeals to like, Josephus gives us an enthusiastic account of Joseph, one of the Tobiads, and his son Hyrcanus (*Ant.* XII. iv). He says of Joseph, "There was now one Joseph, young in age, but of great reputation among the people of Jerusalem for gravity, prudence and justice". When we take his behaviour at the court of Ptolemy and his merciless raising of taxes in that part of Palestine and Syria under Egyptian rule into consideration, it seems clear that he was a consummate hypocrite, and there is no evidence that his sons were any better.

Joseph rose to great riches and power at the expense of the high-priest Onias II (*c.* 245–220 B.C.). Josephus gives us a very unattractive picture of the high-priest, but we have no other evidence by which to check it, and it is highly probable that it is derived from the source that gave him the story of Joseph, and that it was reinforced by his admiration for Joseph.

Whether out of deep personal conviction, or political wisdom, or a combination of the two, Onias' son and successor as high-priest, Simon II (his name is often written Simeon), put himself at the head of the anti-Hellenists who were zealous for the Torah and the old ways. In the light of what the future was to bring, it is well to point out that those who looked to Simon II as leader were far from being a unitary group.

Ben Sira, writing after his death, breaks into a wonderful eulogy on him (50 : 1–21). The most remarkable feature of it is that it is the concluding portion of the long section beginning, "Let us now sing the praises of famous men, the heroes of our nation's history" (44 : 1), which lists most of the outstanding names from Enoch to Nehemiah, but strangely enough omits Ezra, which suggests a certain independance of his views. Though 49 : 14–16 serves as a sort of formal division between the Old Testament worthies and Simon, it is so slight, that it is clear that Ben Sira considered him a worthy successor.

The Synagogue gave him equal honour, when it gave him the exceptional title of *ha-tzaddiq*, "the Just". In *Pirqe Abot* (1 : 2) we are told, "Simon the Just was of the remnants of the Great Synagogue. He used to say: By three things is

* Further details may be found in F. F. Bruce, *Israel and the Nations*, Oesterley & Robinson, *A History of Israel*, Vol. II.

the world sustained: by the Law, by the (Temple-) service, and by deeds of loving kindness".

Though virtually all modern Jewish scholars, except those who feel compelled to handle Talm⸱ dic tradition with kid gloves, agree that Simon the I st was Simon II (*c.* 220–195 B.C.), earlier misunderstandings are still often met. Josephus mentions Simon the Just as high-priest in the early Ptolemaic period and makes him out to be the grandson of the Jaddua who was an older contemporary of Alexander the Great. Unless we maintain that Josephus was drawing entirely on his imagination—not that he knew much of the period—we must exclude the Rabbinic linking of Simon with Alexander as impossible, the more so as it knows that his son (in reality his grandson) built the temple in Leontopolis in Egypt about 163 B.C. The fact is that the rabbis grossly underestimated both the length of the Persian and of the earlier Greek period. They filled the former with the Great Synagogue, the founding of which they attributed to Ezra. Whether or not such a body ever existed, the rabbis did know that the man who had transmitted the traditions that had come down from Ezra's pupils in the early days of the rise of Hellenistic influence was the high-priest Simon. Thereby he probably saved Judaism as we know it. Hence the honorific title of "the Just" and Ben Sira's eulogy; hence too the extreme stress of the Qumran sect on the claims of the house of Onias to be the true high priests.

When Onias III took his father's place, he followed his religious policy. He seems, however, to have been a less efficient political leader. He was constantly slandered by Simon, the captain of the Temple, if not a descendant of Tobias at least a supporter of the Tobiads. He found himself mistrusted by the Jews and so seriously suspected by Seleuchus IV (187–175 B.C.) that he finally felt compelled to go to Antioch to clear his name.

The Abomination of Desolation

From this point on we are fortunate in having far more historical details preserved for us. Both 1 and 2 Maccabees come from the second half of the 2nd century B.C., and the former is a document of high value. For the following period Josephus is a most important witness, though his statements have sometimes to be taken with considerable caution.

Before Onias was able to clear himself with Seleuchus, the king was assassinated by his chancellor Heliodorus. The assassin was in turn swept away by the late king's brother Antiochus IV, commonly known as Epiphanes, for he claimed to be *theos epiphanes*, i.e. god manifest, for he looked on himself as an incarnate manifestation of the Olympian Zeus. True, this claim was made only later in his reign, but it shows the mentality of the man who was to influence the future of the Jews and of Judaism so deeply.

Antiochus was a passionate champion of Hellenism as a way of life, and he was wise enough to see that it was the only force that could hold together a kingdom that had been so severely shaken by the Romans' victory over his father, Antiochus III, at Magnesia (190 B.C.), and was now threatening to crumble away in his hands. So it is easy to see that a man like Onias, a representative of the old ways and an enemy of the Hellenists, would find little favour in his eyes. When Jason (Hebrew Joshua), Onias' brother, offered 440 talents of silver for the high-priestly office, and another 150, if he were allowed to introduce Hellenistic institutions into Jerusalem, Antiochus found two of his greatest desires meeting. He was in perpetual need of money and he longed to further Hellenism. So Jason returned to Jerusalem as high priest.

The replacement of the legitimate high priest by a man with very different ideals must have grieved the pious very deeply. The grief turned to shock, when they saw young men of the best families going about in broad-brimmed hats—a worshipper wearing such a hat could not touch the ground with his forehead, when prostrating himself!—and even more when they were seen exercising stark naked in the new gymnasium. Shock changed to frenzy, when it was found that some of these naked athletes were undergoing an operation to hide their circumcision.

"To be naked and unashamed was one of the glories of the cultivated Greek. It astonished (and still shocks) the barbarian. When Agesilaus, the Spartan king, was fighting on Persian soil he caused his Oriental captives to be exhibited naked to his men, that they might have no more terror of the great king's myriads. Alone among civilised peoples of the earth the ancient Greek dared to strip his body to the sun."* The Asiatic and above all the Semite recoiled from nudity in shame. The Greeks, with their worship of the body beautiful, regarded circumcision as mutilation. That is why it was prohibited by the Roman emperor Hadrian (c. A.D. 130), a prohibition which led to the Bar Kochba revolt.

When the writer to the Hebrews said, "One does not take the honour (of high priest) upon oneself, but is called by God" (4:4), he was writing as a Jew. Normally in Hellenism no such concept existed. Hence Antiochus could not imagine that he was giving offence by replacing Onias by his brother Jason. When Menelaus (Menahem), the brother of the Simon who had made so many difficulties for Onias, sought to outbribe Jason, the king looked on the colour of his money and did not ask about his qualifications. The Greek text of 2 Macc. makes him out to have been a Benjamite, though perhaps related to the high-priestly family by marriage, but in the Old Latin translation he belongs to an inferior priestly family. In either case the head of the Jewish religion was now a man without any claim to the position. He quickly showed that morally too he was a disgrace to the office he had bought. He bribed one of Antiochus' high officials to have Onias murdered, even though he had taken sanctuary in the sacred precincts at Daphne, near Antioch. Then he instigated his brother Lysimachus to steal some of the Temple vessels. This led to a popular riot in which Lysimachus was killed. Menelaus was able by bribery to keep his position (2 Macc. 4:39–50).

Had all this happened during the Persian period with its relatively peaceful internal conditions, it might very well have led to a schism, which would have divided the pious from the Temple and its hopelessly corrupt rulers. As it was, international tensions and Antiochus' mental instability—his enemies called it madness—led to developments, many of whose repercussions are still with us.

* J. C. Stobart, *The Glory That Was Greece*, p. 91.

In 2 Macc. 3 we read how, as a result of the intrigues by Simon the Tobiad, Seleuchus IV ordered his chancellor Heliodorus to raid the treasure of the Jerusalem temple. In spite of the protests by Onias, Heliodorus insisted on entering the Temple with his bodyguard. Because of the prayers of priests and people angelic intervention scattered the bodyguard, threw down Heliodorus and scourged him severely. Whether the story is a popular exaggeration of a man turning back at the last moment because he was gripped by awe, or whether the Jerusalem priests knew more about it than they were prepared to make public, we may be certain that an attempt was made to raid the Temple treasures and that it failed. The people's confidence that God's hand was over His own sanctuary must have been greatly strengthened.

In 169 B.C. Antiochus waged a successful campaign in Egypt, but news of an unexpected reverse at the moment when victory seemed complete was magnified in Judea into a report that he had died. Jason took advantage of this to try and oust Menelaus from Jerusalem. He was only partially successful, for his rival was able to maintain himself in the citadel. Many seem to have perished in the fighting. When Antiochus returned from Egypt, he assumed, reasonably enough, that it had been rebellion against him. He marched on Jerusalem and Jason fled for his life, vanishing ignominiously from the pages of history.

Antiochus entered Jerusalem apparently without opposition, but treated it as though it had been in rebellion against him (1 Macc. 1 : 24), though the estimate of eighty thousand victims (2 Macc. 5 : 13, 14) is probably a gross exaggeration. Still worse, guided by Menelaus (2 Macc. 5 : 15)—but did the wretched man have any choice?—Antiochus entered the sanctuary and stripped it of all its treasures (1 Macc. 1 : 21–24). The unsuccessful attempt by Heliodorus only a few years earlier made the shock of this outrage the greater for the pious, for it seemed to demonstrate that God had turned His face from them because of their sins. The author of 1 Maccabees may well be quoting a contemporary imitation of Lamentations, when he wrote:

> Great was the lamentation throughout Israel;
> rulers and elders groaned in bitter grief.
> Girls and young men languished;
> the beauty of our women was disfigured.
> Every bridegroom took up the lament,
> and every bride sat grieving in her chamber.
> The land trembled for its inhabitants,
> and all the house of Jacob was wrapped in shame (1 : 25–28 NEB).

Even worse was to come. The following year in Egypt Antiochus met with a rebuff by the Romans which probably turned his mental instability into madness. At any rate, when he arrived back in Antioch and heard that the Jews for the most part refused to recognize Menelaus as high priest, he regarded it as an insult and rebellion. In 167 B.C. he ordered Apollonius, governor of Samaria and Judea, to deal with the turbulent city of Jerusalem once and for all. He seemed to come in peace but captured the city on the Sabbath. Many of the inhabitants were butchered; much of the walls was thrown down, and a new citadel dominating the Temple was built. This seems to have been manned by Greek soldiers and some of the supporters of Menelaus.

A decree was made prohibiting the practice of the distinctive features of the Jewish religion. 1 Macc. 1 : 41 suggests that it was a command for the universal Hellenization of religion. While this has perhaps been too readily denied by modern scholars, there is no doubt that it was aimed in the first place at Judea; there is no Jewish tradition that any effort was made to enforce it in the Eastern dispersion or Asia Minor. Finally in the December of that year (167 B.C.) the Temple was dedicated to the worship of the Olympian Zeus, the lord of heaven, and his image, "the abomination of desolation", was placed on the altar of burnt offering. The intention was, of course, that the Jews, who had long been accustomed to call Jehovah the God of heaven, should identify Him with Zeus in the manner favoured by Hellenistic syncretism. Shortly afterwards the leading citizens of Jerusalem were forced to join in a festival of Dionysius (Bacchus). Not content with this the Greeks and their Hellenizing sympathizers tried to destroy all the copies of the Torah; families circumcising their children were punished by death, and royal representatives went round the country towns calling on all leading citizens to sacrifice to Zeus.

Many of the rigorous upholders of the Law tried to withdraw into the wilderness until the troubles were past, but the massacre of nearly a thousand who would not defend themselves on the Sabbath, when they were attacked (1 Macc. 2 : 29–38), showed that passive resistance was insufficient. Heb. 11 : 37, 38 is primarily a tribute to the martyrs of this period. When an old priest, Mattathias of the family of Hasmon, opposed the order to sacrifice to the gods of Antiochus, killing both a Jew who had done so and the officer who was superintending conformity to the king's commands in Modin, Judea exploded.

The story of the long struggle that followed lies outside the scope of this book. The main details can be found in the two Books of Maccabees as well as modern histories of the period. It is a story of extreme heroism and base treachery, of deep trust in God and of much worldly wisdom. Though it was probably not fully realized at the time, its successful outcome was due more to the internal weakness and divisions of the Seleucid kingdom than to the bravery and strength of the Jews. While it was possible only by God's aid, too much was read into this, and the resultant religious nationalism was the cause of most of the misery that was to follow.

The Temple was cleansed and rededicated on the third anniversary (164 B.C.) of the day when the abomination of desolation had been set up. After a fluctuating struggle Judea was finally recognized as independent in 142 B.C. Two years later Simon, the last survivor of Mattathias' sons, was recognized by "the Jews and their priests . . . as their leader and high priest in perpetuity until a true prophet should appear. He was to be their general, and to have full charge of the temple . . ." (1 Macc. 14 : 41, 42 NEB). Far more important than the details of the political struggle were the religious developments, some of which are only now becoming clear. The most important can be briefly summarized.

The Hellenists

It is a very great pity that no record of the views and hopes of Jason and his friends, or even of Simon and his brother Menelaus, has come down to us. We know of them only from the hate-filled distortions of their enemies in 1 and 2 Maccabees and to a less extent Josephus. Menelaus, like his brother Simon, seems to have been primarily a political adventurer, for whom religion was only a means to an end, but it may well be that most of the Jewish Hellenists were genuinely fascinated by the new horizons opened up for them by Hellenism, and that they genuinely thought they were enriching their ancestral religion by its insights. We have only to remember the influence of Hellenistic thought for good or ill in the development of Christianity and we shall pause before judging and condemning too hastily. They were, however, caught up in the hurricane of political events they neither created nor controlled, as were the "German Christians"—the term was used of a group within the Protestant Church in Germany—under Hitler, or many Arab Christians in the present day. They were swept from unorthodoxy into apostasy, without their willing it. When they were hated as apostates they reacted with an even deadlier hatred. With the triumph of the orthodox they were either massacred or had to disappear among their heathen neighbours. From then on Jewry was intellectually and spiritually lamed by the creation of a barrier only the exceptional Jew could openly cross until modern times. They may have left some slight legacy to the Sadducees, but if they did, it is not likely to have been important.

The Nationalists

There seems little doubt that when the national hope of the returned exiles was disappointed by the death of Zerubbabel, it became eschatological, i.e. most did not expect the setting up of a political kingdom of Israel until the Day of Jehovah should come, when He would set up His kingdom upon earth. This damping down of national ardour was the more natural because the major part of the nation had remained in the Eastern dispersion. It was easy enough to transfer Isaiah's picture of Cyrus as the Lord's anointed to his successors on the Persian throne.

Antiochus IV changed all that. Foreign rulers were shown to be the beasts they are depicted as being in Dan. 7. Very many Jews felt that even the best of them could never be trusted again. All religious Jews could explain the plundering and desecration of the Temple only by Israel's sin. For some of them it now became axiomatic that the root sin was acquiescing in foreign rule. To bow down to a foreigner and idolater was akin to denying the kingship of Jehovah. One of the outstanding features of the Maccabean struggle is that while some of the most pious were ready to accept Greek overlordship once their religious rights were guaranteed, the sons of Mattathias battled on even when they could have come to honourable terms. Even though we should make some allowance for personal ambition, which was later to degrade a Hasmonean priest-king like Alexander Jannai to the level of the pagan rulers around him, it is clear that national independence was seen by them and many others as the accomplishment of God's will.

This attitude lived on and reached its climax in the Zealots and Bar Kochba who between them destroyed both Jerusalem and its temple and the Jewish community in Judea. The rise of political Zionism has shown that, even when it was stripped of its religious motivation, this concept never ceased to find a home in the Jewish subconscious through all the long centuries of dispersion.

We shall see, however, that once the Hasmonean priest-kings had been discredited, morally and politically, then the old eschatological hopes revived, expressing themselves very largely in apocalyptic literature. By the time of Jesus most had accepted that if there was to be national independence once again, it would have to be through direct Divine intervention, in all probability through the coming of the long-promised Messiah.

The Hasidim

Suddenly, without any explanation, we are introduced in 1 Macc. 2 : 42 to the Hasideans, a name which today is almost universally identified with the Hebrew Hasidim. The term *hasid*, derived from *hesed*, i.e. covenant loyalty and love, is used thirty-two times in the Old Testament; it is sometimes applied to God, but more often to men. It is found only in poetical passages, most of them liturgical, which suggests that it was a word firmly rooted in the Sinaitic covenant. This means that the AV, RV renderings saints, godly, holy, etc., miss its real meaning. RSV follows the old tradition, but in rendering eight times "faithful" or "loyal" it reveals that its translators knew the true meaning. Apart from two exceptions in the historical books, due doubtless to careless final editing, NEB uses only covenant terms in its renderings, its favourites being loyal or faithful servants. There can be no doubt that it is essentially correct, and that loyalty to the Law, and so to Jehovah, was how the Hasidim understood the name they had adopted.

We have already seen how Jerusalem was twice captured when its enemies attacked it on the Sabbath and how nearly a thousand Hasidim allowed themselves to be massacred rather than take up arms and defend themselves on that day (1 Macc. 2 : 29–38). When Mattathias and his men decided that they would fight in self-defence on the Sabbath, but only in self-defence (1 Macc. 2 : 41), it was doubtless the beginning of the principle that has played such a role in normative Judaism, that since the Law was given that man should *live* by it (Deut. 4 : 1, etc.; cf. Gal. 3 : 21), all commandments, except those prohibiting idolatry, murder and adultery, may be suspended when man is faced by death.

Men such as these could not possibly doubt that the sacking and desecration of the Temple had been due to Israel's sin, which consisted above all in the fact that the Law had not been kept aright. In the face of the fact that they themselves had sought to keep it fully and perfectly it was clear to them that this was not enough. While a righteous remnant might save Jewry from exile and the break-down of society, true blessing could come only when the sinners had been rooted out of Jacob.

The manner in which this was to be accomplished was open to differences in interpretation, and these in turn led to at least one major split within the ranks of the Hasidim. It will be best, however, to consider this in the setting of the short-lived period of independence under the Hasmonean priest-kings.

The Resurrection Hope

All serious scholarship agrees that while the hope of the resurrection is to be found in the Old Testament, the number of passages that contain it are few. Even in such late works as Qohelet (Ecclesiastes) and Ben Sira it is not mentioned, which can only mean that it had no vital importance for their authors. Yet, when we come to New Testament times, two centuries later, it is virtually taken for granted, cf. Jn. 11:23, 24. What the resurrection of Jesus Christ was to do for His followers was to change a strong hope into a certainty. When we examine the Old Testament passages that indubitably speak of resurrection or fully conscious life after death we find that they all spring from the spiritual anguish and need of those to whom the light was given.

So, too, it was in the Maccabean period. Those who suffered most and perished most frequently were from among the best elements of the people. They were too conscious of their own shortcomings to think of themselves as the Suffering Servant of Jehovah, as did apparently the men of Qumran at a somewhat later date. To these men and women in their agony the Holy Spirit brought the assurance of a life to come that would redress the wrongs of the present. We have no indication how it came, whether through some men of outstanding spiritual stature, or as a sudden realization of the truth among the pious as a whole, as has happened more often in the history of the Church than many realize.

It is worth mentioning that the Hebrew Scriptures know nothing of "the immortality of the soul", and theologians today have come reluctantly to the recognition that the concept is not to be found in the New Testament either. It could not well be, for the Biblical concept of man is that he is soul, formed by the union of spirit and body (Gen. 2:7). Without a body man cannot have true life, but at the best a shadowy existence.

The immortality of the soul is essentially a Greek concept and the only extant Jewish writing from this period in which it is found is the Wisdom of Solomon, written in the essentially Greek city of Alexandria about 100 B.C. Josephus' ascription of a belief in immortality of the soul to Pharisees and Essenes (*Ant.* XVIII. i. 3, 5; *War* II. viii. 11, 14) is best understood as an adaptation of their belief in the resurrection to Greek concepts. Philo of Alexandria (1st cent. A.D.) strongly upheld the immortality of the soul while rejecting the resurrection of the body. Some two hundred years later the rabbis had reached an uneasy compromise between the two views. Today though the resurrection of the body is still the official teaching of orthodox Judaism, most Jews believe rather in the immortality of the soul which needs no body, if they look for an after-life at all.

It is symptomatic that the one group that did not accept this hope, at least publicly, was the one to which the name Sadducee was later to be given. The explanation of them that best fits the evidence is that they were predominantly members of the professional priestly families. Most of the priests were on duty at the pilgrim festivals and for two extra weeks in the year. For the rest of the time they lived away from Jerusalem and augmented their incomes in any way that was consistent with their standing. On Temple policy they had no influence. There were, however, those groups which lived in Jerusalem, which filled the administrative offices in the Temple and which to a great extent ·dominated its policy and the council later called the Sanhedrin. Some of them will have been involved in the intrigues of Jason and Menelaus and have been swept away with the Hellenizers. Most, however, will have held aloof. They were conservatives, concerned with preserving the privileges of the priesthood and the traditions which had been handed down to them over many generations. For them Ezra's policy will have been unwelcome, because it gave increased importance to the layman. The dreams of the Hellenist will have been abhorrent, because they ran counter to ancient tradition. Very many of this group will have been able to ride out the storm better than most, and changes in the high-priesthood will have made little difference for them. Both their smaller degree of suffering and their innate conservatism will have closed their minds to what they regarded as a novel doctrine of resurrection. It was not until the Hasidim were able to influence national policy that the Sadducees emerged as a political party as well.

13

GROWING TENSIONS

There is every reason for accepting as correct the account in 1 Macc. 14:25–49 of the appointing of Simon as high priest and civil leader—in fact, it speaks of confirmation, not appointment, since he already effectively held these offices. The account, however, even though it is probably derived from a contemporary document, is too late to reflect the feelings of those who proposed and accepted this agreement. We can, therefore, reconstruct the scene only from our imaginations.

Doubtless there were many present who re-echoed the psalmist's words, "When the Lord restored the fortunes of Zion, we were like those who dream. Then our mouth was filled with laughter, and our tongues with shouts of joy" (126:1, 2). They will have believed that the days of the Messiah were about to break in on them. This is borne out by the willingness in some circles to think in terms of a Messiah from the tribe of Levi, e.g. Jubilees, Testaments of the XII Patriarchs (though it is not clear how far the influence of Qumran is to be seen here). Doubtless those who so thought tended to expect that the Messiah would be a son or descendant of Simon.

Others, however, and among them many of the more spiritual elements among the people, must have had their misgivings and doubts from the first. There had been so much in the Maccabean struggle which had exhibited human nature on a very low level alongside those that had sanctified the Name by their sufferings and death. Indeed, the position was very similar to that of the modern State of Israel. There are many today, even in Israel, who genuinely and in all good faith question whether the setting up of the state can have been the expression of God's will because of the many evil acts and injustices that accompanied it.

The sequel showed that there were some who were most unhappy about Simon's position as high priest. From the time that Solomon had deposed Abiathar from his position as joint high-priest the position had descended from father to son among the descendants of Zadok, and Ezekiel had taught that only this family had a right to function as priests (40:46, etc.). Though Ezekiel's teaching was not accepted after the return from exile, and all who could prove their Aaronic descent were allowed to function as priests, it must have come as a profound shock to find that the proud representatives of the Zadokites had been replaced by the house of Hasmon, whose family tree has not even come down to us.

The shock must have been the greater because Jonathan, Simon's elder brother had been appointed to the post by Alexander Balas, who was a common adventurer claiming to be the son of Antiochus IV Epiphanes. As Oesterley says, "It may be that at the time Jonathan did not realize that acceptance of this high office from such a contemptible usurper was derogatory to the office itself; and probably if he had it would have made no difference—the end was too important to him to care about the means—but in looking back one cannot fail to see that the whole transaction was rather sordid".*

It could be that Simon's succession to Jonathan as high priest would have been widely questioned, had Onias IV, the legal heir to his father Onias III as high priest, not fled to Egypt after Menelaus had instigated his father's murder. There he was able to obtain permission from Ptolemy VI to build a temple after the Jerusalem pattern at Leontopolis in the eastern delta.† Here the same ritual as in Jerusalem was carried out by Zadokite priests until after the destruction of the Jerusalem temple in A.D. 70 (*Ant.* XIII. iii. 1, 3; *War* VII. x. 2–4), when it was closed on instructions from Vespasian.

We know very little about this temple, for none of the dominant groups in Palestine had an interest in publicizing it. We do not even know how far it was patronized. There does not seem to be any evidence that the synagogue community in Alexandria was interested in it. At the same time it should be clear that it would not have continued for over a century had there not been a considerable number of worshippers.

Though Onias IV had forfeited the allegiance and admiration of the legitimists, that did not mean that they were satisfied by Simon and his successors. Already before the Qumran discoveries Oesterley could write in 1932, "Nevertheless, as the subsequent history shows, it is certain that a great undercurrent of feeling against the Hasmonaean High-priesthood among a very considerable section of the anti-Hellenistic Jews was already running at this time."‡ The discoveries at Qumran have revealed that the basic motivation for the existence of the movement was its dissatisfaction with the Jerusalem high priests, whom they considered to be illegitimate because of their descent and manner of life.

The next shock was caused by Simon's son and successor John Hyrcanus. He was a good ruler, even though the first six years of his reign were troubled ones. Shortly after his accession in 134 he was attacked by Antiochus VII. He held out in Jerusalem for a year but had then to become tributary. Judea did not become completely free again until 128, when the Seleucid king fell in battle. This must have opened the eyes of many to see that the Messianic age was further off than they had hoped. It was not this, however, that led to his rupture with the Hasidim, or Pharisees, as Josephus now calls them, even though he had been their disciple. The story is found in *Ant.* XIII. x. 5, 6. It is not easy to understand, but the only reasonable explanation is that Hyrcanus had in fact assumed the royal power, even though we do not find this directly attested

* *A History of Israel*, Vol. II, p. 252.

† This suggests that the leading priests did not interpret the Law of Moses as demanding one sanctuary only.

‡ *op. cit.* p. 266.

before his son Aristobulus I.* The Pharisees could condone his high-priesthood, though they disliked his combining that office with leadership in war, but for him to claim kingship was to fly in the face of God's choice of the house of David. There is no evidence that there was any known Davidic claimant to the throne; the Pharisaic objection was purely, so far as we know, on principle.

Hyrcanus turned his back on the Pharisees and accepted the policies and outlook of the Sadducees. In itself this was quite natural and might have happened in any case, for in his position as High Priest he must have been brought into very close contact with this group of priestly traditionalists. In addition he probably had often to chafe under the burden of Pharisaic interpretations of the Torah, which must have complicated the burden of government. The results, however, were far-reaching.

At the time when Hellenism was making its inroads in Judea the position of the Hasidim seemed almost desperate, even when they were headed by the high priest Onias III. During the Maccabean struggle they were clearly willing to submit to foreign overlordship so long as they were allowed complete freedom of worship. Under Hyrcanus, however, they were allowed to influence national policy—we do not know how it was under Simon—and power went to their heads. When they saw power passing to the Sadducees, they became for the time being as much a political party as a religious one.

It may well be that in writing of them as Pharisees, Josephus is indicating that the Hasidim had already split. It seems difficult to believe that the priestly traditionalists we find later at Qumran could ever have co-operated as closely with John Hyrcanus as it is clear the Pharisees did to begin with.

The Teacher of Righteousness and Qumran

Ezra's reforms contained within them an unresolved element of ambiguity. What was he really stressing in his enforcement of the Torah? It is usually assumed that the Torah was uppermost in his mind. But we saw earlier what care he took that those who returned with him should be representative of all Israel. This tension may be briefly expressed by putting two Rabbinic passages side by side. "If it were not for My Law which you accepted, I should not recognize you, and I should not regard you any more than any of the idolatrous nations of the world" (R. on *Exod.* 30:11–34:35). "R. Hananiah b. Aqashya said, 'God was minded to give merit to Israel. Therefore He multiplied to them Torah and commandments, as it is said, It pleased the Lord for His righteousness' sake to make the Law large (Isa. 42:21)" (*Mak.* 3:16). While these two passages are not contradictory, it is clear that the main weight of the first is on the Torah, of the second on Israel. We should probably be near the truth, if we suggest that the men of Qumran stressed the former, the Pharisees the latter, though probably neither side recognized that the tension was there.

Among the Hasidim there were apparently those who were prepared to let Israel perish provided the Torah was kept strictly and without compro-

---

* The story is dealt with in some detail by Oesterley, *op. cit.* pp. 282–287; a similar view is taken by a number of Jewish writers, e.g. L. Finkelstein, *The Pharisees*, pp. 762f. and literature cited there.

mise—more fairly put, they were certain that God would intervene before Israel was destroyed. Others, however, stressed that the Torah was given that men might live by it. They were willing, if necessary, to suffer martyrdom, but for the sake of Israel they were prepared to moderate the demands of the Torah, though they doubtless expected that it would finally be kept perfectly.

The men of Qumran seem to have belonged to the former group. The Pharisees were prepared to compromise with the manifest shortcomings of Simon and John Hyrcanus in the hope that they might gently be led into better paths. The men of Qumran called them "speakers of smooth things", because they were willing to call black grey in the hope that the grey might some day turn to white. For the other wing of the Hasidim, however, compromise was excluded.

They might have remained no more than a protest, an attitude of mind— there were always a few such among the earlier rabbis—had it not been for a remarkable man whose name has not been transmitted to us and whom we know only by the title "The Teacher of Righteousness". So little do we really know about him, that we are not certain even how his title should be rendered; some suggest "the rightful teacher" or "the right guide" and that the designation was held by more than one man. Be that as it may, we are clearly dealing in the first place with a definite historical individual.*

Twenty years after the beginning of this movement of protest God raised up a Teacher of Righteousness who taught them the true way of life, for he had been given special insight into the purposes of God, so that he was able to make known to the "last generations" what God was going to do in the "last generation". He clearly believed that God had given him a special illumination and he rejoiced in it. In one of the *Hymns of Thanksgiving* it is doubtless he who says, "These things I know by understanding from Thee, for Thou hast opened my ears to receive wonderful mysteries". In brief, he claimed a Divinely given understanding of the prophetic books, which enabled him to recognize the situation he and his followers were passing through and the right course of conduct to follow, a course justified by the fact that they were living in what was clearly the final period before the breaking in of the Day of the Lord.

Over against the Teacher of Righteousness in the Qumran literature there stands the figure of the Wicked Priest. Though other identifications have been suggested, there is little doubt that he was Alexander Jannai, or Jannaeus, who was high priest and king from 103 to 76 B.C. That such a title was given him was not just a mark of prejudice, for though he was a relatively successful ruler, he was by any standards a bad man. The activity of the Teacher of Righteousness may very well have started in the time of Hyrcanus, but the active evil and opposition of Jannai—we know that he was a persecutor of groups of the pious—caused the Teacher of Righteousness to withdraw with his disciples to Qumran.†

* The first news of Qumran and its scrolls in 1947 was so unexpected that some suspected an elaborate hoax. There is still no unanimity on many points and complete ignorance on others. See F. F. Bruce, *Second Thoughts on the Dead Sea Scrolls*[3] as the best introduction.

† The main ruins at Qumran can be dated in the time of Jannai, but there was already a smaller settlement some time earlier, which could go back to the time of Simon, or possibly even his brother Jonathan, who

Behind this withdrawal lay the concept that Israel had clearly been rejected by God. Not merely was there an inadequate loyalty to the Torah, but the high-priesthood was illegitimate as well as defiled by Jannai's semi-pagan life, and the kingship had been usurped by those with no right to the title. So the group in Qumran, in their own eyes at least, were the righteous remnant, the Servant of Jehovah, and their sufferings bore witness to the validity of their claim.

Our purpose here does not call for a closer investigation of the reason why the community at Qumran differed in various ways from the description given by Philo, Josephus and Pliny of the Essenes, with whom they are normally identified. It may be that others were moved by their example but did not wish to be members of a community so predominantly priestly. Equally we need not ask what proportion of the members lived in Qumran itself. After all Josephus, writing of the Essenes, tells us (*War* II. viii. 4), "They have no one certain city, but many of them dwell in every city." While this almost certainly exaggerates their numbers, it supports the impression that Qumran was their headquarters and rallying place on special occasions.

The main points of importance in their views are the extreme stress laid on physical purity, the most rigorous observance of the commandments, especially those connected with the keeping of the Sabbath, where they went far beyond the Pharisees,* the primacy of the priesthood even over the Messiah expected from the house of David, and the possession of a different calendar. Too much stress should not be laid on a partial sharing of property, ascetic living, and apparently abstinence from marriage by at least some of the members. All these were probably not basic but a consequence of the conviction that they were living in the last days.

In some ways the calendar is perhaps the most significant of the points mentioned. It automatically separated them from the official religion of Jerusalem, because by it the great feasts and the fast of the Day of Atonement fell on other dates than in the calendar followed by both Sadducees and Pharisees and maintained to this day. The calendar is the one demanded by the books of Enoch and Jubilees, which are probably older than the Qumran movement itself. Whether this calendar was ever used we do not know, but it seems that the concepts behind it are old, and have, perhaps, left their traces on the Old Testament. It seems clear, however, that the men of Qumran believed that it was ancient and willed by God Himself. By adopting it they proclaimed both their continuance of ancient tradition and their loyalty to God.

It must remain an open question whether sacrifices were brought at Qumran, or whether they considered that when God permitted His temple to be polluted, it implied the end of sacrifice for the time being.

We need not be surprised then that the men of Qumran play no part in the New Testament. Even John's baptism will have repelled them, for the accept-

---

died in 142 B.C. This fits with the statement that the Teacher of Righteousness came some twenty years after the beginning of the movement.

* A small and isolated community can always apply rules of behaviour more strictly than those who mingle freely with their fellow men.

ance of the multitude and their baptism on no more than verbal repentance with no period of probation went against their most cherished principles. But when Jesus of Nazareth was prepared to consort with the scum of society, with the Quisling tax-collectors and harlots, He had placed Himself outside any serious consideration as a teacher of the truth. It may be noted also that He did not use any of the far-fetched prophetic interpretations of Qumran.

Even though Qumran and its adherents lived on the fringe of Palestinian life, they had a far-reaching influence on Jewry as a whole. The ancient priestly traditions they represented, the strictness of their keeping of the Torah, the asceticism and purity of their lives, all raised them far above any normal censure. That they could disassociate themselves from the Temple and its sacrifices helped to undermine its authority. In spite of their high position the Sadducees were seen as those who had been untrue to an older priestly tradition. Even though the Pharisees made the keeping of the Law humaner than did the Qumran tradition, the ordinary man, who was in any case no friend of undue strictness, saw the possibility of questioning Pharisaic authority. In other words Qumran represented not a heresy, but an unhealable schism which weakened all religious authority.

This helps to explain why the religious leaders, whether priestly or rabbinic, found it so difficult to deal with Jesus. There was no all-powerful authority that could silence Him. Equally, when the Church appeared on the scene after Pentecost, it demanded tolerance in a society which had already had to tolerate a schism which the authorities probably considered fundamentally more dangerous.

It is worth adding that there is fairly wide agreement that the Qumran survivors of the destruction of Jerusalem in A.D. 70 were drawn to the Church. If that is so, it will go far to explain the rise of the Ebionite heresy among the Hebrew Christians towards the end of the first century.

14

THE SLIDE TO RUIN

When Aristobulus I, son of John Hyrcanus, died in 103 B.C. after a brief reign of only a year, it seemed as though the future of the Jewish state was guaranteed. The Seleucid kingdom of Antioch was so torn by struggles between rival claimants to the throne, that once Antiochus VII (Sidetes) had died, there was nothing to be feared from there. John Hyrcanus had occupied Idumea, i.e. that part of southern Judea that had been settled by Edomites, and offered the inhabitants the choice of accepting Judaism or exile. Later he captured Samaria, destroying the temple on Mt. Gerizim, but he did not interfere with their religion otherwise. Aristobulus occupied Galilee and part of Iturea in the foothills of Lebanon. Here too the inhabitants were given the choice of Judaism or exile. This policy was to be followed later by Alexander Jannai, at least in some of his conquests. It was not dictated either by fanaticism or political motives alone. In all these areas part of the population stemmed from the poorer Judean and Israelite elements that had not gone into exile, so there was a considerable knowledge of the Mosaic revelation diffused among the people. This, and the conviction that Palestine, both the original Judean territory and the areas conquered by the Hasmonean priest-kings, was Jehovah's land made conformity easy for the majority. Since, however, there is no suggestion in first century A.D. Jewish sources that heathen beliefs and practices had lingered on in these areas, it seems probable that Judaism had been quietly making its way both in Idumea in the south and Galilee in the north quite a time before their conquest.

The Hasmonean rulers could not foresee that they were providing some of the high explosive that was to destroy the second Jewish commonwealth.

Alexander Jannai (103–76 B.C.)

Alexander Jannai, or Jannaeus, was Aristobulus' eldest brother. He was a man filled with the joy of battle and the lust for conquest. When he died, his territories stretched down the Mediterranean coast to the frontiers of Egypt, thus making Philistia Jewish for the first time. East of Jordan he had captured most of the Decapolis as well as Gilead and the ancient territories of Moab as well as part of northern Edom. Yet his acquisitions had been dearly bought. He suffered four major defeats, and some of his victories were almost as costly in lives as his defeats. His forces consisted mainly of mercenaries, whose support necessitated heavy taxation. For six years he was involved in a bitter civil war, and it was finally only the fear of foreign domination that rallied his subjects to him.

Though defeat and heavy taxation played their part, the chief reason for his unpopularity was religious. It was not deliberate on his part, but he acted as the catalyst to bring the growing tensions and divisions among the people to a head.

From all the accounts we have of him, it is hard to believe that he had much, if any, genuine religion. He was essentially "a man of blood", and it offended every genuine susceptibility that such a man should function as high priest. In addition he had married Aristobulus' childless widow, Alexandra Shelom-Zion or Salome. While this would have been justified by the law of levirate marriage (Deut. 25 : 5–10), it was expressly forbidden to the high priest (Lev. 21 : 13, 14, cf. Ezek. 44 : 22). The ruling in the Mishnah, "The king . . . may not contract levirate marriage nor may his brothers contract levirate marriage with his widow" (*San.* 2 : 2), is probably intended to rule out the possibility of any repetition of his action on the plea that the king took precedence over the priest. The bitter dislike shown by some of his subjects against him as priest is shown by the fact that in the year 90, when he was preparing to officiate at the altar during the feast of Tabernacles, he was pelted with the *etrogim* (citrons) the festival pilgrims were carrying and insulted by shouted insinuations against the legitimacy of his birth. He displayed his character by turning his guards loose on the demonstrators. Josephus claims that about six thousand were killed (*Ant.* XIII. xiii. 5).

All this was rendered even worse for some by his support of the Sadducees, a policy inherited from his father. It will be remembered that this was more or less forced on John Hyrcanus, because the Pharisees objected to his having assumed the position of king.

As we saw in the previous chapter, this led the Teacher of Righteousness and his disciples to withdraw to Qumran and to abandon the political community as beyond hope of regeneration. The Pharisees and their supporters, on the other hand, decided to fight, even though some of their number will have tried to hold aloof. It was probably in this period that the support of the common man, who had little interest in religious parties, switched decisively to the Pharisees. Quite apart from other weaknesses the Sadducees had become compromised by their close association with the hated King Jannai.

Josephus estimates that 50,000 Jews were killed in the fighting that followed (*Ant.* XIII. xiii. 5). The ill success of the rebels caused them to call in Demetrius III of Antioch to their help. The very magnitude of Jannai's defeat at Shechem caused a revulsion of feeling among the more nationalistic. Demetrius withdrew and the Pharisaic party was crushed.

Jannai's revenge was terrible. Let Josephus tell how he dealt with the captured leaders. "As he was feasting with his concubines, in the sight of all the city, he ordered about eight hundred of them to be crucified, and while they were living ordered the throats of their children and wives to be cut before their eyes" (*Ant.* XIII. xiv. 2). We need not be surprised that some eight thousand of the survivors chose voluntary exile until after the king's death.

There is some excuse for Jannai. His father had disliked him, possibly with good reason, and had shown his feelings by designating his younger brother Aristobulus as his successor. He had grown up in Galilee, where he had received a thoroughly Hellenistic, i.e. largely pagan, education. Contemporary kings probably commended his strong-arm methods.

S. Zeitlin summarizes the reason for the Pharisaic opposition as follows:

> They believed he had made Judaea a secular kingdom. They regarded him as a Hellenistic ruler who was a Judaean only by birth. They also opposed his conquest of new territories and his forcing of the inhabitants to accept Judaism. This, to them, was a travesty of religious belief. The Pharisees favoured proselytism, but only by propaganda and teaching, not by force. Furthermore they feared that the conquest of new territories, inhabited by Syrians and Greeks, would have a demoralizing influence on the Judaeans.*

The Pharisees might believe that it was wrong to spread Judaism by force, but they had yet to learn that they must not impose their views on their fellow-Israelites by similar methods. Some of the more spiritual will have learnt from the disaster that had struck them, but most were embittered and bided their time until they could hit back at those who had smitten them so grievously.

Alexandra Salome (76–67 B.C.)

On his death-bed, because of the youth of his sons, Jannai passed the throne on to his wife. Josephus is probably correct in saying that he advised her to "put some of her authority into the hands of the Pharisees". If tradition is correct, and there is no reason for doubting it, she was the sister of Shimon ben Shetah, one of the Pharisaic leaders, and so she needed no urging to carry out her husband's advice. Indeed she so handed over authority to the Pharisees, that Josephus could say, "She had indeed the name of the ruler, but the Pharisees had the authority" (*Ant.* XIII. xvi. 2).

It is comprehensible that the Pharisees could not restrain their desire for revenge. The Sadducees found their traditions set aside, traditions of a religious nature sincerely held and for the most part probably far older than those of the Pharisees, who in this period seem very often to have been the innovators, even if the innovations were often religiously wise and progressive. The greater the loyalty of a Sadducee to Jannai had been, the more his life was in danger. Their leader, Diogenes, and others were murdered by the Pharisees. In estimating such accusations, it should not be forgotten that Josephus, our authority, was himself a Pharisee.

What the outcome might have been need not be speculated on. The future was shaped by the fact that the queen's elder son, Hyrcanus, was a supporter of the Pharisees, while the younger, Aristobulus, was regarded by the Sadducees as their only hope. This division in outlook was no mere natural by-product of the rivalry between the brothers but was an expression of their character and outlook. Hyrcanus, as the elder, had become high priest and was the heir apparent. He was a quiet and unambitious man, and there is no evidence from his tragic life that he desired high position. Aristobulus, however, showed his father's character, and the queen was merely recognizing the facts of the situation when she appointed him commander in chief of the army.

When the ageing queen was confronted with a Sadducean deputation,

* *The Rise and Fall of the Judaean State*, Vol. I, p. 328.

which included Aristobulus, which claimed that their existence was being threatened, she allowed them to occupy some of the most important fortresses in the country. This would, almost certainly, have brought civil war, then and there, had the queen not been fortunate enough to die at the ripe age of seventy-three after nine years on the throne.

The queen's favour had made the Pharisees not merely ministers and lawmakers but also the judges. So later generations, dominated by the Pharisaic outlook, looked back to her reign as the golden age of Hasmonean rule, the more so as the land had at long last rest from war. In addition we may well assume, since there is no evidence to the contrary, that it was only on the Sadducees and not on the common people that their hand lay heavily. The Talmud relates that under her rule, "the grains of wheat were as large as kidneys, the grains of barley like olive-kernels, and the beans like golden denarii" (*Taan.* 23). The bitter truth is that even a much stronger ruler could not have averted the sorrows to come; she made them certain.

For all that, to whomever the credit should be given, her reign was the Indian summer of the period that had started so gloriously with the heroic struggle against Antiochus Epiphanes. It was natural, therefore, that men should look back to this period with longing and that even nature should be credited with exceptional bounty. We find the same, when many in Britain look back to the allegedly halcyon days of Edward VII and Queen Victoria.

Hyrcanus II and Aristobulus II (67–63 B.C.)

Hyrcanus automatically followed his mother on the throne, but Aristobulus was able almost immediately to collect an army and attack him. When the armies met near Jericho, so many of the royal troops deserted to Aristobulus, that Hyrcanus fled to Jerusalem. When his brother followed him, he gave up both crown and high-priesthood, probably with great relief, on the sole condition that he could enjoy his personal estate so long as he did not meddle in public affairs.

Well would it have been for him and for the Jews, if he had been allowed to follow his natural desires and to sink into obscurity. But just because Aristobulus was the champion of the Sadducees, who had returned to power through him, many of the Pharisees looked to Hyrcanus to restore the favoured position which they had enjoyed under Queen Salome.

The decisive influence came, however, from another source, viz. a wealthy Idumean called Antipater. As the father of the famous, or infamous, Herod the Great he has shared in the glorification or vilification of his son. Hence all statements about his birth are suspect. S. Zeitlin sums up all that can be said with reasonable certainty:

> The chief schemer to place Hyrcanus back on the throne was Antipater, whose father, also named Antipater, was the *strategos* (military governor) of Idumaea at the time of Jannaeus Alexander and Salome Alexandra . . . Antipater was born in Idumaea and was a Judaean by religion. Whether his father was one of those Idumaeans whom John Hyrcanus I had given the choice of accepting Judaism or going into exile, or simply a native Judaean who had settled in Idumaea, makes no difference to

his religious status. According to the view of the Pharisees, a person whose ancestors were proselytes was a Judaean of equal religious status with a native of ancient lineage. Only the Sadducees held otherwise.*

If Antipater the elder was really a proselyte, he must have been an exceptional man to obtain such an important position. It seems more likely that he was a Jew by birth. This seems the more likely because other stories were invented to cast discredit on Herod's birth.

There is little to be gained by speculating about Antipater's reasons and motives. F. F. Bruce is probably correct, when he says:

> At any rate, Antipater was one of those men who are wise enough in their generation to realize that it is much more important to have the substance of power than its titles. His idea was that Hyrcanus should regain the titles of power in order that he himself, as the power behind Hyrcanus' throne, should enjoy the substance.†

Antipater joined hands with Aretas III, king of the Nabateans, whose interest it was that a weak king should sit on the throne in Jerusalem. Both brought pressure to bear on Hyrcanus to convince him that his life was in danger from Aristobulus. Though there is no grain of evidence to support this, so many brothers of kings in that period met a premature and violent end, that Hyrcanus can be excused for believing the worst about Aristobulus' intentions. Finally he fled to Petra, Aretas' capital. Aretas placed a large army at his disposal at the price of twelve cities, which had earlier been captured from the Nabateans.

Aristobulus was heavily defeated and besieged in Jerusalem. So deep had the party spirit gone, so bitter were the feelings it had aroused, that many Jews went down to Egypt. Josephus (*Ant.* XIV. ii. 1) calls them "the principal men", which here probably means the more devout, who placed godliness before the support of party. The supporters of Hyrcanus laid hold on an old man, Onias "the Circle-maker", famous for his power in prayer. They brought him to their camp outside Jerusalem and demanded that he curse Aristobulus. When threatened with death he prayed, "O God, King of all the people, since those standing beside me are Thy people, and those who are besieged are Thy priests, I beseech Thee not to hearken to the others against these men, nor to bring to pass what these men ask Thee to do to these others". His reward was to be stoned to death.

If at all possible, worse was to come. The besieged priests needed sacrificial animals for the Passover sacrifices. They offered high prices for them, but the money was received and the animals withheld. The Talmud adds the picturesque detail that the besieged discovered that the one animal they were hoisting up was a pig (*Men.* 64) and that God showed his displeasure by an earthquake. The more moderate account by Josephus that God "sent a strong and vehement storm of wind that destroyed the fruits of the whole country, till a modius of wheat was then bought for eleven drachmae", in other words more than the famine price given in Rev. 6:6, is more likely to conform to reality, the more so as the wind was probably an aggravated example of the

---

* *op. cit.*, pp. 344f.
† *Israel and the Nations*, p. 178.

sha'arav, or *hamsin*, which so often blows at that time of year and is capable of doing severe damage to the crops.

There was no future now for the Hasmonean kingdom, but God mercifully shortened the days of anguish by bringing in the Romans. They had become involved in the area by their war against Mithridates. When Pompey's lieutenant Scaurus came to Damascus, he heard of the troubles in Palestine. Drawn like a vulture to the prey, he marched there to see if he could turn matters to Rome's and above all his own advantage. Both sides appealed to him, offering him large bribes; he decided in favour of Aristobulus. Two years later (63 B.C.) Pompey decided to settle matters himself. Aristobulus aroused his suspicions and then tried desperately to defy the Roman power. When Pompey appeared outside the walls of Jerusalem, he thought better of it and surrendered to the Romans. The supporters of Hyrcanus opened the gates of the city to the Romans, but some of Aristobulus' followers resisted in the Temple for three months.

Finally on a Sabbath, which may well have been the Day of Atonement, it was stormed. Josephus estimates the Jewish casualties at 12,000, but he is seldom trustworthy, when he is dealing with high numbers. The priests on duty allowed themselves to be cut down as they carried out their duties. Pompey entered the Holy of Holies only to find to his surprise that it was empty. The Jews were probably equally surprised, when he spared the Temple treasures, but this was the only token of mercy shown to Judea. The ring-leaders of the opposition were executed, though Aristobulus was spared. Judea lost the Greek cities of the coastal plain and its control over Samaria and Transjordan. What was left became a vassal of Rome.

The Religious Situation

For the devout, Pompey's entry into the Holy of Holies must have been as serious a blow as Antiochus Epiphanes' desecration of the Temple just over a century earlier (169 B.C.). They could interpret it only as a sign of God's deepest displeasure.

Those who had withdrawn to Qumran must have seen it as a vindication of their policy and of the teaching of the Teacher of Righteousness, and many must have shared their view. We cannot doubt that the Pharisaic leaders were sickened by the blood that stained their hands and the desecration of the Name to which they had contributed so much. Doubtless they were represented among those who asked Pompey that Judea might revert to its former status under the high priests without political independence (Josephus, *Ant.* XIV. iii. 2). Certainly they rapidly developed an increasingly pacifist policy.

Among the people in general two tendencies began to develop rapidly, tendencies which were in themselves not incompatible. The Hasmonean successes had stirred Messianic hopes. Their collapse made many believe that this was merely the necessary preliminary to the coming of the Messianic deliverer, the darkest hour before the dawn. In addition there was a growing conviction that not devotion to the Torah but to the national liberty of the people was God's prime desire. It does not mean that those who later became known as the Zealots were opposed to the Torah, but that they considered that what they held to be the welfare of the people of God took precedence over the observance of the law of God, should any clash between them arise.

Whatever the origins of the Synagogue, it was the degradation of the Temple and its services under Jannai that first made it a power in Palestine. Whereas it had been a centre for the study of Torah and a kind of substitute for the Temple for those who could not go there, it now began unofficially to replace the Temple in men's affections. This was not overt and deliberate, but an expression of the deep revulsion felt by many. Since the Sadducees could not be expected to favour such an attitude, the leadership in most synagogues slipped into the hands of the Pharisees, though this is truer of Judea than of Galilee.* They welcomed this for the opportunity it gave them of teaching their views, and this made them, as we find in the New Testament, the most respected of the religious teachers. The ordinary man might well seek to dodge the stricter rules they made, but he would seldom challenge their decisions. In practice, especially in Galilee, their main rivals were the Zealots, not the Sadducees.

ADDITIONAL NOTE

The Synagogue

The origins of the Synagogue are in fact wrapped in obscurity. There are some, mostly Jews, who would trace them back to the period of the monarchy, but most scholars confidently place them in Babylonia during the exile. It is fair to suggest that their confidence is equalled only by their lack of evidence. It was pointed out in ch. 2 that the conditions for it, or for any other major religious development, were far from propitious. Particularly important is that no evidence for the existence of the Synagogue, even in an embryo stage, can be found in Ezekiel, or in those parts of Isaiah which most scholars place in the exilic and immediately post-exilic periods.

Before we can argue for even the first beginnings of the Synagogue, we have to bring evidence for reasonably regular religious activities unlinked with a sanctuary, which at least in theory were open to all Israelites. In spite of the lack of much positive evidence, we may reasonably assume that in both priestly and prophetic circles small groups will have met from a very early date from time to time for study, discussion and prayer, but we cannot deduce any continuing tradition from this.

The earliest certain mentions of the Synagogue come from Egypt from the period 247–221 B.C. Against this we have to set their non-mention in Esther and Tobit. The latter's silence is particularly important because of the picture it gives of Jewish piety in the Eastern dispersion in the late Persian period, cf. p. 61. In fact the only certain pre-Christian mentions in Jewish literature are Enoch 46:8; 53:6, probably early first century B.C. The Gospels and Acts are sufficient evidence that both in Palestine and the Western dispersion the Synagogue had become a regular feature of communities both large and small by

* Geza Vermes, *Jesus The Jew*, pp. 55ff.

the time of Christ. A passage like Acts 15 : 21 shows that they had existed long enough to be taken for granted.

Wherever and under whatever conditions the Synagogue may have started, we can be reasonably certain that it had little influence until it had been accepted in Jerusalem and Judea. There the foundation for it must have been laid by Ezra's work, which demanded that all male Jews must know something of the Torah. It was pointed out in ch. 8 that Ezra had separated his reading of the Torah from the Temple courts (p. 47). No one can doubt that a necessary sequel was the setting up of a "school", where the implications of the Torah were studied by the scribes and the leisured. With this agrees the considerably later tradition, which attributed most of the older Rabbinic regulations to the men of the Great Synagogue, the founding of which was looked on as Ezra's work. Clearly this was not a synagogue but a house of study (*bet-ha-midrash*) for the intensive study of the Torah. This is often confused with the Synagogue, because at a later date it might well be held on synagogue premises, and later still served as a synagogue for those who studied there. There is little evidence for its existence in the time of Christ outside Jerusalem and a few centres in the Eastern dispersion.

The Synagogue proper will have begun as an answer to the need of teaching Torah to the ordinary man. Its services were originally confined to the Sabbath and centred round the reading and exposition of the Books of Moses, but a reading from the Prophets and a simple service of worship were soon added. The services were then extended to Mondays and Thursdays, the traditional Palestinian market days, and then gradually daily prayers became the norm. This was doubtless taken over from the house of study. That attendance was not compulsory is shown by Luke's remark that Jesus went to the synagogue "as His custom was" (4 : 16). Both for our Lord and Paul their recorded synagogue visits are always on the Sabbath.

Apparently there was an attempt to link the Synagogue with the Temple worship. Though few details are known, it seems that the country was divided into twenty-four districts to parallel the twenty-four orders of priests and Levites. They were expected to send their "lay" representatives to Jerusalem for a week at a time to share in the national worship. Those who were unable to go were expected to have special prayers in the local synagogue. If this system really functioned, it will have played a considerable part in the development of the regular synagogue prayers.

There is ample evidence that the Synagogue did not become really prominent in Palestine until about 100 B.C. There will have been two main reasons for this. The proselytizing of Idumea and Galilee by force made the teaching of the Torah to the new Jews a matter of real urgency. Then also the same excesses of the Hasmonean priest-kings, which caused the Qumran community to withdraw to the desert, will have caused the ordinary religious man to prefer the atmosphere of his home synagogue led by honoured members of the local community.

Apart from Jerusalem and Rome there was normally only one synagogue for a Jewish community. Alexandria came to have more than one, but they evidently would have preferred to have only the one. It was so big, that it is claimed that men with flags had to signal when the congregation was to say Amen—with a more or less fixed liturgy the failure to hear was not so important. In places where the Jewish community was predominant the seven men who headed the community were also responsible for the synagogue, and the building served as the community school house as well. Even where the Jews formed only a minority, they were expected to build and maintain a synagogue.

Normally a synagogue had only three officials. The ruler of the synagogue was always one of the most respected members of the community. He was responsible for seeing that qualified persons read, led in prayer and expounded the portion which had been read. Then there was the controller of alms, who had to see to the needs of the poor, sick and suffering. Finally there was the attendant, who had to look after the scrolls, keep the building clean and maintain order. He might well be the schoolmaster as well. All three were chosen on the basis of personal merit and not of birth or wealth. While a synagogue would welcome the presence of a man well versed in the Torah, this was not essential; if such a man, later dignified by the title Rabbi, was available, he was not one of the officials. Indeed, as may be seen even today, the only power he possessed for enforcing his rulings came from the quality of his life and character.

When the Temple and its priesthood vanished, the local synagogue offered a rallying point for the community. Its fairly fixed liturgy and generally accepted methods of understanding the Torah meant that no very great divergence grew up between community and community or country and country. For a few centuries Jewry officially longed for the rebuilding of the Temple and the restoration of sacrifices, but little by little the Synagogue came to be accepted as the ideal.

15

THE LONG SHADOW OF ROME

The immediate effect of Rome's intervention in Palestine was to reduce the Jewish kingdom (Judea) to little more than a rump state. It was made dependent on the Roman governor of Syria and had to pay a heavy tribute. Hyrcanus II was allowed to continue as high priest and civil head of state, but he lost all those territories won by the Hasmoneans where the Jews did not form the majority of the population, viz. the whole coastal plain, most of Samaria, the Decapolis, which included Scythopolis (Bethshan) west of Jordan. All that was left to Hyrcanus was Judea (including Idumea), Perea, the stretch beyond Jordan from south of Pella to the Dead Sea, and most of Galilee, which was, however, isolated territorially from the south.

From many points of view the Jew had much to gain. Religiously his territory had lost most of its heathen and sectarian (Samaritan) inhabitants, and so Judaism could have developed without much fear of heathen corruption. Then there was peace for the first time since 168, if we ignore the nine years of Alexandra Salome's reign. The heavy tribute to Rome—Josephus says above ten thousand talents "in a little time"—must have been far less than the cost of incessant warfare and the upkeep of an extravagant court.

Longer term implications showed themselves more slowly. Persia's conquests under Cyrus and Cambyses enlarged the geographical area forming the background of the Jews and of Biblical history, but did not fragment it. The same is true of Alexander's conquests. Even the frequent wars between the Ptolemies and Seleucids do not seem to have had much effect on Jewish unity. Indeed, these wars in large measure had much of the nature of civil war. The position changed drastically with the Roman take-over of the Seleucid empire, or rather of the remains of it in Syria, for the eastern portion had fallen into the hands of the Parthians, who became Rome's main enemy in the East. Not until the third century A.D., apart from a brief interlude in A.D. 115–117, was Rome able to push its frontier east of the Euphrates and to incorporate Mesopotamia into its empire. This meant that Judea was separated from the Eastern diaspora by a hostile frontier, and this, in turn, greatly increased the importance of the Western diaspora.

The tension between Rome and the Parthians largely cut the age-old trade routes of the Near East and so strengthened the magnetic pull of the city of Rome. Though the saying "all roads lead to Rome" and its earlier formulations do not seem to have a Roman origin, they express a historical fact. Throughout the Roman empire old trade routes, unless they served the commerce of Rome, became secondary. Hence under the shadow of Rome Palestine became a dead end, for the traffic between Egypt and Mesopotamia had lost much of its importance. That is the main reason why Rome treated Judea as it did other isolated areas and allowed it to be ruled by nationals whom it could trust. Hence it never experienced the advantages of the best Roman rule; when finally it had to come under direct rule, those employed were generally third-rate material, interested mainly in self-enrichment.

The Rise of Antipater

We cannot identify with certainty the circles that had sent a deputation to Pompey in 63 B.C. asking for the same position under Rome as they had enjoyed under Persia and the Greeks before the Hasmoneans came to power. Presumably they represented the more important priests and elders and some of the wiser Pharisees; it is not impossible that Qumran also had its delegates. They were prepared to surrender all political freedom provided they had complete religious freedom and autonomy. They had learnt in one way or another through the fiasco of the Hasmoneans that political freedom was not to be won by man's wisdom and strength. The bulk of the people, however, regarded the Hasmonean dynasty with almost as much veneration as their ancestors had the Davidic kings, and they were prepared to die for it. Though they recognized Hyrcanus II as legitimate ruler and high priest, they could not help realizing that he was little more than a puppet of the Romans, and that Antipater exercised the real power in their interest.

In 57 B.C. Alexander, son of Aristobulus II, raised a revolt without much success. The result was that Hyrcanus was deprived of civil power, and the country was divided into five districts governed by "an aristocracy" (Josephus, *War* I. viii. 5). The next year Aristobulus and his other son Antigonus escaped from Rome and raised a revolt, which was quickly suppressed. In 55 B.C. Alexander, encouraged by the absence of the Roman legate, had another try, which was equally unsuccessful. The defeat and death of Crassus at Carrhae at the hands of the Parthians in 53 B.C. led to a revolt by a military leader who had espoused Aristobulus' cause, but again it was quickly suppressed. According to Josephus' estimate the number of men killed and enslaved must have exceeded 50,000, to say nothing of the losses among the Jews serving Hyrcanus and the Romans.

Throughout this troubled time one man stood unwaveringly on the side of the Romans. Antipater did all he could to help them, both in their general campaigns and in their suppression of the revolts in Judea. He may have been motivated by his knowledge that only under Hyrcanus could he hope for power and position, but there can be little doubt that he recognized, as did Josephus a little more than a century later, that Rome was bound to triumph. It might not be very interested in what might happen in Judea, but it could not afford to risk the Parthians gaining a foot-hold there.

When civil war broke out between Julius Caesar and Pompey in 49 B.C., Antipater first aided Pompey, whose generals were in control in Syria, but after Pompey's decisive defeat at Pharsalus, he threw all his weight on Caesar's side. When Caesar found himself in difficulties in Egypt, Antipater's help was of great value to him. All this had been done in Hyrcanus' name, so he was confirmed in the high-priesthood and given the title of Ethnarch, one step below King. Permission was given for the restoration of the walls of Jerusalem. Taxes were remitted, religious freedom confirmed, in matters concerning Jews alone they were to be judged by their own courts, they were freed from military service and Roman troops were withdrawn. Jewish territory in the coastal plain and Galilee was increased, and the port of Joppa was returned under special terms. Even the tribute for Joppa was remitted in the Sabbatical year. Wide-reaching privileges were given to Jews in the diaspora, who were put officially under the protection of the high priest. Perhaps most important for the future was that Judaism became a *religio licita*, which enabled the Synagogue to spread to the extent we find in the New Testament. Details of Caesar's decrees are given by Josephus (*Ant*. XIV. x. 2–8), though the text is generally held to be in poor condition.

The use of the term *religio licita* in such a context is strictly speaking an anachronism.* What Caesar did was to arrange for "the senate to exempt synagogues from a general ban on associations".† He also confirmed the freedom of worship and the autonomy of Jewish communities in Phoenicia and Asia Minor. This helps to explain why Paul always tried to make his first public appearance in the synagogue of the towns he visited.

We need not wonder that the Jews mourned Caesar's death as greatly as they had rejoiced over Pompey's, which they regarded as God's judgment on him for having entered the Temple.

It is not easy to give the reasons why the Jews should receive such favoured treatment. They were never liked by the Romans who may in part have been merely continuing a situation they found in existence. More likely Caesar realized that in their dispersion the Jews formed an alien element, which would not so easily take the side of their neighbours, should they rebel.

Antipater's reward was that he was made procurator of Judea and a Roman citizen, and was relieved of taxation. Julius Caesar had realized that Hyrcanus was merely an indolent, weak and largely unwilling figurehead, and that Antipater was Rome's best and most trustworthy friend. While Judea had not reverted to its status under Simon the Hasmonean of *socius*, i.e. ally of Rome, it was free of taxation by Rome, while it had the right to impose its own.

While Judea could not have avoided being involved in the turmoil that shook the Roman world after the assassination of Julius Caesar, it could have enjoyed relative quiet and prosperity with a far wider territory and greater degree of self-government than it had ever had under the Persians. As already pointed out Rome had no real interest in involving itself in Jewish affairs or in annexing the country. It is now that we see the first indubitable signs of the madness that was to destroy the Jewish state in less than four generations.

The hatred of Antipater by his Jewish contemporaries is not easy to understand fully. Even if his father had been an Edomite who had accepted Judaism in the time of John Hyrcanus (as we saw, this cannot be proved), Antipater, the

---

* S. Benko & J. J. O'Rourke, *Early Church History*, p. 256.

† Michael Grant, *The Jews in the Roman World*, p. 58.

son of a Jewish mother, ranked as a Jew without question, except perhaps among the Sadducees. It seems far more likely that the stress on his alleged Edomite origin was merely a motivation for something deeper.

Sadducean hatred is easy enough to understand. Hyrcanus was the champion, at least in name, of the Pharisees, and it was Antipater's refusal to acquiesce in Aristobulus' usurpation of power that had prevented the Sadducees from resuming the exercise of religious power they had enjoyed from the later years of John Hyrcanus to the reign of Alexandra Salome. But what are we to say of the popular attitude supported by many of the Pharisees?

Here Antipater was doubtless in part to blame, for he ceased to hide adequately behind Hyrcanus. Once he had been made procurator he immediately appointed Phasael, his eldest son, governor of Jerusalem, and Herod, his second, governor of Galilee. According to Josephus (*Ant*. XIV. ix. 2) he was only fifteen at the time, but since, when he died about forty-five years later, Josephus claims that he was about seventy (*Ant*. XVII. vi. 1), almost all historians amend the text to twenty-five. Even so it was clear that his appointment was not on merit but intended to strengthen the position of Antipater and his family. This increased the opposition of the rich aristocrats.

Trouble in Galilee

Herod soon ran into deep trouble in Galilee, and indeed from this time on the chief centre of Jewish disaffection was to be found here, though obviously its influence was felt in Judea as well and reached out far into the diaspora. There were two main reasons for this. Unlike the bulk of the inhabitants of Judea, who had known "the yoke of the Law" from the time of Ezra, if not before, most Galileans had taken it upon themselves only about half a century earlier in the time of Aristobulus I. To the ordinary man the idea of nationalism, of being a member of God's chosen people, appealed far more strongly than the Pharisaic careful and minute adherence to the details of the Torah. So even during the first century A.D. Pharisaic influence in the Galilean synagogues was relatively weak, cf. p. 96. The maintaining of the national freedom, which the Hasmoneans had won at such a cost, became a holy duty for many of the Galileans. It could be suggested that they had also had less opportunity of being disgusted by the realities of national freedom as displayed in Jerusalem.

There was perhaps ultimately a deeper reason. There is ample evidence that when Aristobulus conquered Galilee much of the land passed into the possession of large estate owners from Jerusalem and Judea, who squeezed out as much as possible as absentee landlords, a situation mirrored in a number of Christ's parables. As a result the general level of prosperity was much lower than in the South, the number of landless and workless very much higher, cf. the parable of the labourers (Matt. 20: 1–16). In the final struggle against Rome in A.D. 66–70 one of the Galilean leaders John of Gischala would have been called a revolutionary left winger today, though he did not go so far as Simon bar Giora, who was probably a Judean.

A careful reading of the New Testament would suggest that the majority of cases of demon-possession among Jews which are recorded were in Galilee.

This would suggest the extreme tension and misery that existed there.

When Herod came to Galilee, he found that a large band of "robbers" under a leader called Hezekiah was terrorizing not merely Jewish Galilee but also the adjacent Syrian areas. By vigorous measures Herod succeeded in capturing him and many members of his band. He had them all executed. Josephus (*Ant.* XIV. ix. 2–5, *War* I. x. 6, 7) tells us that this gained not only the gratitude of the Syrians but also of Sextus Caesar, the governor of Syria. But "the chief men among the Jews" urged Hyrcanus to call Herod to account, for he "has transgressed our law, which has forbidden to slay any man, even though he were a wicked man, unless he had been first condemned to suffer death by the sanhedrin". The mothers of those who had been executed "continued every day in the temple, persuading the king and the people that Herod might undergo trial before the sanhedrin for what he had done". Hyrcanus felt compelled to comply.

It should be obvious that Hezekiah was no ordinary brigand, and that the inability of the Romans to deal with him satisfactorily was due to his enjoying the sympathy of the local Jewish inhabitants. Even to hit at Antipater through his son the aristocrats of Jerusalem would hardly have taken up the cudgels for ordinary bandits. The fact is that Josephus, who was a great upholder of law and order, regarded religious terrorists as brigands and robbers, cf. the story in *Ant.* XIV. xv. 5. Zeitlin expresses it succinctly: "Galilee at the time of Herod's governorship bordered on Syria, and claimed that many cities on the border rightfully belonged to her. A man named Ezekias, with a group of other Judean patriots, overran the cities, seeking to restore them to Judea. The Romans, who had established the boundaries in the area, looked upon these men as bandits".*

Here we discover that the Hasmoneans had started a fire that could not be quenched. There were many who believed that while a Jew might go and live in the diaspora under heathen rule, if he wished, the soil of Israel was holy, and heathen rule there an abomination. At all costs the foreigner and the Quisling had to be driven out. They were men who had entirely failed to learn the lessons of the exile and, indeed, of the centuries of Persian rule. We have already seen that it is not by chance that we first meet them in Galilee.

This national fanaticism was increased by the effects of poverty. In the hundred and twenty years that had passed between the beginnings of the Hasmonean revolt and Julius Caesar's confirmation of Hyrcanus in religious and civil power the land had been bled white of its best manhood. It had been repeatedly ravaged, and taxes, tribute and bribes had removed its riches. Judea had suffered heavily but the position in Galilee was even worse. Such a combination of religious enthusiasm and grinding poverty normally creates an explosive mixture. Had the Jews been successful in the Great Revolt from Rome, it would almost certainly have brought a major upheaval in society with it.

Let us return, however, to Herod. He realized that the summons to appear before the Sanhedrin was serious. He had Sextus Caesar send a letter to Hyrcanus, who was *ex officio* the presiding judge of the Sanhedrin, demanding that

* *The Rise and Fall of the Judaean State*, Vol. I, p. 372.

he acquit Herod. On his father's advice Herod returned to Jerusalem with a strong body of armed men. On the day of the trial he entered the court in military dress, surrounded by a bodyguard.

By Jewish law Herod was not liable to the death penalty, for he had not personally killed the men. At first it looked as though his show of force would silence the members of the court, but Shemaiah, "a righteous man", demanded the death penalty, warning the court that Herod would execute its members, when power fell into his hands. (Josephus tells us that this forecast was actually fulfilled for all but Shemaiah, whom Herod respected because of his courage). The court would probably have followed his advice, had not Hyrcanus postponed the case, probably on the grounds that the sentence could not be given on the day of the trial.

Herod hastened back to Sextus Caesar, who made him governor of Coele-Syria and apparently of Samaria also, thus making him one of the most powerful men in the area. He marched on Jerusalem to exact vengeance, and it needed the arguments of Antipater and Phasael to make him desist.

Antigonus

The assassination of Julius Caesar in 44 B.C. threw the Roman Empire into a period of chaos, which did not come to an end until 31 B.C., when Octavian defeated Antony and Cleopatra at Actium; Judea was inevitably involved, the more so as the Parthians tried to take advantage of the confusion.

First Cassius and then Antony extorted huge sums of money from the country. A friend of Hyrcanus, Malichus, hoped to replace Antipater as the power behind the throne and so had him poisoned—so most probable rumour had it—in 43 B.C., but Phasael and Herod simply took over their father's place. In 41 B.C. Antony even appointed them joint tetrarchs, which meant that Hyrcanus lost even the shadow of political power. Unfortunately for the Jews Antigonus, the surviving son of Aristobulus II, was standing in the shadows waiting.

When Cassius left Syria in 42 B.C. to meet his end at Philippi, Antigonus tried to win the throne with the help of his brother-in-law, the king of Chalcis, and of the governor of Tyre, but Herod had no difficulty in defeating him. Thanks to Antony's involvement with Cleopatra, the Parthians were able briefly to occupy Syria. Antigonus used their presence to make himself king and high priest in Jerusalem.

It is most doubtful whether he ever had any chance of regaining his father's throne, but his inability to read the situation brought him ruin and death. The Romans might have thrown over the sons of Antipater, had they been convinced that some other Jew would rule the land more efficiently. But for a man who had brought in their worst enemy, the Parthians, there could be neither mercy nor compromise.

Antigonus seized Hyrcanus and Phasael by treachery, but Herod, being suspicious, was able to save his life by flight. Phasael committed suicide in prison. Antigonus mutilated his uncle Hyrcanus, so that he could no longer function as high priest, cf. Lev. 21 : 17–21; he either "bit off his ears with his own teeth"

The Long Shadow of Rome

(*War* I. xiii. 9), or "he cut off his ears" (*Ant.* XIV. xiii. 10). Even if we query Josephus' former version, the very fact that it existed shows the reputation Antigonus had among his contemporaries.

After considerable vicissitudes Herod reached Rome, where he was wel-comed by Antony and Octavian; they caused him to be declared king of the Jews by the Senate. Since he was already engaged to Mariamne, grand-daughter of both Hyrcanus II and Aristobulus II, this gave him some claim to the throne, though less than Aristobulus III, Mariamne's young brother. It will depend largely on our estimate of his character, whether we believe that this was his goal all along, or whether, as Josephus says, he was hoping that the crown would be given to his brother-in-law, in which case he would have played the same role as Antipater had under Hyrcanus, the more so as Aristo-bulus was far too young to be an efficient ruler. Josephus' statements about Herod are hard to evaluate. Sometimes he is simply repeating the statements of Nicolas of Damascus, Herod's court historian. At other times he is torn be-tween loathing and admiration. In a case like this he is likely to be giving the facts.

It took Herod three years to win what the Romans had given him. Finally, besieged in the citadel of Jerusalem, with his kingdom ruined, Antigonus fell at the feet of Sosius, the Roman general helping Herod, and begged for mercy. He did not yield to Herod because he knew that his hands were stained with Phasael's blood and so he could expect no mercy. Sosius called him Antigone, a coward and a woman, and took him in chains to Antony in Antioch. Josephus tells us that Herod bribed Antony to put him to death. Since, however, Dio Cassius tells us that Antony had Antigonus scourged while bound to a cross, a punishment "which no other king had suffered at the hands of the Romans", before having him beheaded, Zeitlin may well be right when he says, "The inhuman punishment expressed Antony's scorn, not only for Antigonus the king, but towards the Judaeans and their religion, of which Antigonus was high priest."* It may be true that Herod had bribed Antony, but it is probable that the money was not needed. The Romans knew that a warning and example to the petty rulers along their eastern frontier was needed, in case others also might be tempted to have dealings with the Parthians.

Aristobulus III and Mariamne were to play their part in Herod's domestic troubles along with their mother Alexandra, Hyrcanus' daughter, but the death of Antigonus meant the effective end of the house of Hasmon. It had brought forth deliverers for Israel, whose name should be held in honour, but power had corrupted it, and in its corruption it corrupted Israel also. For those who had eyes to see, none could now lead Israel into the paths of peace apart from the Messianic King from the house of David, but the sight of Israel was so corrupted that few recognized Him when He came.

---

* *op. cit.*, p. 411.

16
THE JEWISH DISPERSION

We are told in Acts 2 that on the day of Pentecost there were in Jerusalem visitors from the east, from Mesopotàmia, Media, Parthia and Elam, then from the north and north-west, from five areas of Asia Minor, Cappadocia, Pontus, Phrygia, Pamphylia and the Roman province of Asia; from the wider Mediterranean world Egypt, Libya, Crete and Rome were represented; finally from the south some had come from Arabia. Obviously this list is not intended to be exhaustive, for it does not mention Syria with its large Jewish population, or Greece, but it does give some idea of how widely the Jews had spread in the century before the birth of Jesus. They stretched from the west coast of India to the south coast of Gaul and probably to the major ports in Spain.

The number of Jews in Arabia at the time was probably small, and they did not come into prominence until the time of Mohammed, when those in the area under his control were either driven out or annihilated, apart from the few who accepted Islam. This was due to special reasons at the time and did not express the normal tolerant attitude of Islam to the Jews. Since Arabian Jewry had little influence on Judaism as a whole, it need not be considered further.

The Eastern Dispersion

It can only be regarded as remarkable that we know virtually nothing of the history and conditions of the large number of Jews living in Parthia and Media during the first century B.C. We may reasonably assume that the picture given us in *Tobit* of a hard-working and pious community often troubled by its neighbours (cf. pp. 61, 96) still held true. It has been pointed out that both in the period when Palestine was under Ptolemaic rule and even more when it was absorbed into the Roman sphere of influence, there was a hostile frontier separating Judea from the eastern dispersion. This must not be exaggerated. Josephus' description of the importance of Nehardea and Nisibis for the collection of Temple taxes—the half-shekel—and gifts (*Ant.* XVIII. ix. 1) rings true. His account suggests, however, that local unrest restricted the number of pilgrims, and that those that risked the long journey went in large caravans for self-protection. It was this lack of "law and order" which increased the Jewish tendency to become town-dwellers in Mesopotamia and Persia.

One interesting result of these disturbed conditions was the setting-up of what was essentially a semi-autonomous Jewish state for a few years in Babylonia. Josephus tells us with considerable pleasure of the exploits of Asineus and Anileus and claims that their power lasted fifteen years (*Ant.* XVIII. ix. 1–9). Power, however, corrupted and finally destroyed the brothers. On their death the local inhabitants rose against the Jews and massacred many of them.

A more responsible character, Zamaris, left Babylonia at the head of 500 mounted archers. Herod the Great settled him in the far north of his kingdom to control the trade routes from Damascus and protect them from the wild men ·of Trachonitis. Both he and his descendants seem to have been very popular and successful, and they created an important centre of Jewish population drawn mainly from the Eastern dispersion (*Ant.* XVII. ii. 1, 2).

Evidence for the living contact between Babylonia and Jerusalem may be found in Herod's calling of Hananel from there to be his high priest (p. 112). Common sense suggests that he must have been well known in Jerusalem and acceptable to most of the priestly leaders there.

Perhaps the best illustration of the links between the East and Judean orthodoxy is offered by Hillel. He had studied Torah in Babylonia, though the name of the school or schools has not come down to us. As a mature man he came to Jerusalem about the middle of the first century B.C. to study at the feet of Shemaiah and Abtalion, the acknowledged leaders of the Pharisaic party. After some years he returned to Babylonia, but before the end of Herod's reign he was back in Jerusalem and was soon recognized as leader of the more liberal wing of the Pharisees, especially as he could speak in the name of his two great teachers. His story shows that the Pharisaic leaders in Jerusalem accepted the qualifications given by schools in Babylonia, when former students came to Jerusalem for higher Torah studies. Equally it shows that the provincial could be more liberal than those at the centre.

Historically, the main importance of the Eastern dispersion was its offer of a solidly traditional background for Palestinian orthodoxy, which was constantly being threatened by the infiltration of Greek thought, and of a refuge, when Palestinian Jewry was smashed by Roman power and the growth of Christianity.

There is not much evidence for Jewish missionary work in the area. The chief exception was Adiabene, a small vassal-kingdom of the Parthians in the north of Mesopotamia. Josephus gives us the story how its king Izates, his mother Helena and his whole family were converted to Judaism (*Ant.* XX. ii–iv). Their tombs are still extant in Jerusalem a short distance to the north of the old wall. It seems clear that the local Jews, if there were any, had nothing to do with his conversion, which was very unpopular among the nobles of Adiabene.

Jews in Asia Minor

There are no reasons for doubting Josephus' statement that Antiochus III (223–187 B.C.), after he had won Palestine from the Ptolemies (p. 69), caused his general Zeuxis to send two thousand Jewish families from Mesopotamia and Babylonia to Lydia and Phrygia, where there had been plots against him, because he knew he could count on Jewish loyalty (*Ant.* XII. iii. 4). Because they were not simply voluntary immigrants, they were given many communal rights and often full citizenship in the cities in which they were settled. His successors followed the same policy, and Sir W. M. Ramsay has argued convincingly in his *Cities of St. Paul* that if Paul was a citizen of Tarsus, it meant that one of his ancestors was settled there with full citizen rights about 170 B.C. by Antiochus IV, when he changed the city's constitution.

It may be that because full citizenship brought them into closer contact with their Hellenized, pagan fellow-citizens, it may be because they were moved so suddenly to an ancient area of Greek culture, they were more than most out of touch with Jerusalem. Here, and virtually here alone in the dispersion, we find evidence for the syncretistic influence introduced by Hellenism (pp. 70, 79), though it may be that modern scholars place too sinister interpretations on the evidence, which may have been little more than an olive-branch to their pagan fellow-citizens. After all, no one takes the pagan depiction of the sun-god in his chariot found in mosaics from Galilean synagogues as evidence for a syncretism which undoubtedly did not exist at the time. Some pagan influence, however, there was, and Acts 19:13-19 gives some evidence for this. It may also explain Paul's stress on the fact that he was "a Hebrew born of Hebrews" (Phil. 3:5), i.e. the language of his home in Tarsus was Hebrew or Aramaic, not Greek. Probably there was a greater acceptance of the Gospel by Jews in this area than anywhere else. The opposition of many of them mentioned in Acts may have been due as much to the fear of losing a favoured position as to religious objections.

All this helps to explain why the Jews of Asia Minor find so little mention in the story of Jewry's last desperate struggles against Rome. They found themselves at home in their surroundings and experienced less dislike from their pagan neighbours than most in the Western dispersion.

Rome

We know little or nothing of the beginnings of Roman Jewry. Perhaps the first Jews to settle there were merchants from Alexandria and Asia Minor. The real growth came as a result of Pompey's interference in Judean affairs, when so many of his Jewish prisoners of war were sold as slaves. When they obtained their freedom, most lived on there as poor freedmen. The community must have been severely shaken by two expulsions, the first under Tiberius (*Ant.* XVIII.iii.5) and the second under Claudius (Acts 18:2). The former was the result of a scandal narrated by Josephus, but Philo is probably correct in seeing the anti-Jewish feelings of the emperor's favourite Sejanus as the real cause. Suetonius tells us that the latter was due to internal riots in the Jewish community; most scholars accept that the preaching of Christ lay behind them.

Though in both cases the expulsion order did not stay long in force and may well not have been strictly carried through, their possibility shows us the essential weakness of the community. In addition we have records of eleven synagogues in the city, which suggests its splintered nature. So, here too, while Roman Jewry is of importance in the history of the apostolic and sub-apostolic Church, it did not leave any significant mark on the development of Judaism.

Alexandria

Between the collapse of Persian rule in Egypt in 404 B.C. and Alexander the

Great's conquest of the land in 332 B.C. all known traces of the Jewish communities mentioned in Jer. 44 and of the settlement at Elephantine (p. 23) vanished. There must have been survivors, but they will have merged with the new influx brought in by the Greeks.

When Alexander conquered Egypt, he evidently felt that its age-old communities would not be sufficiently open to the Hellenistic concepts he brought with him. So he built Alexandria, a new city on the Mediterranean, to be mainly Greek in blood and altogether in culture.

Though Josephus, quoting Hecataeus, claims that many Jews joined Alexander's forces (*Contra Ap.* I. 22, cf. *Ant.* XI. viii. 5), there is no suggestion that they were included among the veterans he settled in Alexandria.* Indeed their later anomalous position with massive rights but yet not full citizenship suggests that they were inserted among the original founding members by Ptolemy I. He was able to seize Jerusalem on the Sabbath (*Ant.* XII. i. 1), and took many Jews back with him to Egypt—according to *The Letter of Aristeas* over a hundred thousand—some of whom he placed in garrisons up and down the country; presumably the majority were settled in Alexandria. They were soon joined by others who came because of the advantages offered them. As a result we find at a later date that of the five districts into which the city was divided, two were regarded as Jewish, and they were not confined to them.

Though they were not full citizens, the Jews of Alexandria were in full control of their internal affairs. This need not have caused difficulties, but the additional privileges given them by the Romans aroused jealousy, the more so as these meant that they were relieved of some of the onerous duties falling on others. In addition they were probably never forgiven for the help given to Julius Caesar by Antipater (p. 100) in his conquest of Egypt. Between 38 and 66 A.D. we hear of four riots between Greeks and Jews in Alexandria; in at least the first and last the Jewish community suffered very heavily.

The Greek culture of Alexandria was very mixed. The ancient superstitions and magic of old Egypt and of the Eastern Mediterranean generally mingled with the mystery religions and theosophical and gnostic concepts from India. At the same time, however, it was one of the few great centres of Hellenic culture. Here the educated Jew met the philosophical thought of Greece at its best.

Since the Ptolemies were always tolerant towards Judaism, and the Romans who followed them were normally indifferent, there was never the violent reaction to Hellenistic thought that Antiochus Epiphanes caused in Judea. There were many who opened themselves to Greek thought that they might then offer the riches of Judaism to their neighbours in terms they could understand. An example is the Wisdom of Solomon (c. 100 B.C.) in which Hebrew wisdom is offered in terms the Greek might understand and with the adoption of the idea of the immortality of the soul, which is opposed to Old Testament concepts. Philo (died c. A.D. 50) is an example of the Jewish Bible student who tried to harmonize it with Greek thought.

The very large number of Greek words taken up into Rabbinic Hebrew as shown by the Mishnah and Midrashim gives some idea of the influence the

---

* R. L. Fox, *Alexander the Great* (p. 198) says "perhaps too a contingent of Jews," but gives no evidence.

Western dispersion in general and Alexandria in particular had on the rabbis in Palestine. It went far to reduce the impact of the reaction to the policy of Antiochus Epiphanes.

In the history of religion, however, Alexandrian Jewry's greatest contribution was its translation of the Old Testament into Greek, popularly known as the Septuagint (LXX). From at least the time of Ezra (p. 48) it became general practice to translate the portions of Scripture read in public into Aramaic, the language of ordinary life. Though a tradition must have grown up rapidly, it was not allowed to write down and read this translation. So it must have remained fluid for centuries. The same must have happened in the Western dispersion, only that Greek was used. In Egypt and particularly Alexandria this was gradually felt to be inadequate. Greek friends who visited the synagogue found the translation often crude and noted its variations. So a written translation, first of the Pentateuch, then of the Prophets and Psalms and finally of the Writings was undertaken. The whole operation was completed by c. 50 B.C.

Beyond pointing out that the story told in *The Letter of Aristeas*, that the translation of the Pentateuch was made at the command of Ptolemy II (285–246 B.C.) by seventy-two translators sent from Jerusalem, is mere fantasy, we need not concern ourselves with the history of the LXX.* It is quite likely, at least for the Pentateuch, that what we now know as the LXX is in fact a revision of an earlier translation. What is important is that for the first time the revelation of God became accessible to the Gentile world divorced from the language in which it had originally been given. Until the early Christian Church adopted the LXX and based its controversy on renderings in it, which might not really express the force of the Hebrew, even Palestinian Jews were prepared to give it virtually equal standing with the original Hebrew. Then, of course, it began to be regarded as the work of Satan, and about A.D. 130 it began to be replaced among Jews by the new translation by Aquila.

The translators of the LXX faced the problems that all Bible translators have had to face. So often a literal translation of the Hebrew carried quite different connotations in Greek. The result was a language which at times differed considerably from ordinary popular Greek, but for those Gentiles who frequented the Synagogue, it was evidently easily understandable, and it provided the basic vocabulary for the messengers of the Gospel as they went out into the Greek-speaking world. Before the Church took the upper hand, it is probable that the influence of the LXX lay behind a large majority of those who joined the Synagogue or who were reckoned among the God-fearers.

---

* Full information and discussion may be found in Paul E. Kahle, *The Cairo Geniza* (1947) and Bleddyn J. Roberts, *The Old Testament Text and Versions* (1951).

17
HEROD THE GREAT

There are few characters in ancient history more difficult to evaluate than Herod. This is partly because we know more about him, and especially about his private life, than we do about most comparable persons. What is worse, this information is often self-contradictory and almost always biased. This is because it is derived either from Nicholas of Damascus, Herod's court historian, who was extensively used by Josephus, or from those who hated him most bitterly on religious, nationalistic, or personal grounds, cf. also p. 102.

We should do well to remember that the Qumran Covenanters left their settlement after an earthquake in 31 B.C., i.e. at a time when Herod was firmly on the throne, and did not return there until after his death. More than that, Josephus (*Ant.* XV. x. 5) tells us that "from that time on Herod continued to honour all the Essenes", because one of them, Menahem, had told him when he was still a child, that he would be king, and later, when this came true, he foretold a long reign. If we are to identify the Essenes with Qumran, as do the vast majority of scholars, it would be a strange thing, if they were to return to public life, if Herod had really been the monster he is so often depicted as being; it is even less likely that they would have given him the possibility of honouring them.

Religious hatred of Herod was based mainly on the fact that the head of the Jewish state was no longer the high priest, unless indeed it was mainly Zealot in motivation. Klausner has well expressed the reasons for the nationalistic hatred:

By the time that Herod "the Great" came to the throne (37 B.C.E.) not only the royal city, but the entire land of Israel, was a wilderness. During the thirty years which had elapsed from the death of the queen Shelom-Zion (Alexandra Salome) till Herod became all-powerful (67–37) far more than a hundred thousand Jews were killed. All these were the pick of the nation, the healthiest, mainly the young men, and the most enthusiastic, who had refused to suffer the foreign yoke.

Thus the nation was enfeebled to the last degree. It no longer contained men of bold courage for whom political freedom was more precious than life; there remained only those whom we have described—the bitter-minded and the fervid of faith, who did not shrink from martyrdom for the sake of the Law. And even these, ere long, Herod had crushed by force.

There remained no longer the possibility of a great, popular rising which should venture forth, sword in hand, to meet the usurper, a foreigner by birth and depending upon foreigners for support.*

Except for the refusal to accept Herod as a Jew, we can look on this descrip-

* *Jesus of Nazareth*, pp. 1444f.

tion as essentially accurate. It betrays the bitterness of the modern dedicated nationalist, who could bring himself to write, "The Maccabaeans built up a Jewish Palestine: the Herodian kings destroyed it." Klausner could not bring himself to recognize that once Rome appeared in the East, Judea was doomed, and that the rivalry between Sadducee and Pharisee, between Aristobulus and Hyrcanus, only hastened the end. The role of Herod was not to destroy, but to preserve until He whose right it was should come.

When Augustus said, making a Greek pun, that he would rather be Herod's pig (*sys*) than his son (*hyios*), he was putting his finger on that side of Herod's life that has left an indelible blot on his memory. His life was embittered by three ambitious and unforgiving women, one of whom he loved to distraction, and rendered unsure by the plots of his sister and his sons. There can be little doubt that emotionally undermined and physically rotten in his last couple of years, he was no longer responsible for his actions at the time, which included the killing of the baby boys in Bethlehem. The number involved will not have been large—Bethlehem had little importance at the time—and at a time when the lives of many of the religious leaders were being threatened, it will have caused little stir. That is sufficient reason why it was not mentioned by Josephus.

An attempt to end the internecine conflict between Hyrcanus II and Aristobulus II, the two sons of Alexander Jannai, had been made by marrying Alexandra, daughter of the former, to Alexander, the latter's eldest son. Their children were Mariamne and Aristobulus III. Hyrcanus rewarded Herod for his loyalty by giving him his grand-daughter as wife. The Romans were not merely influenced by his loyal efficiency, when they nominated Herod as king in 40 B.C. Aristobulus III was only about sixteen at the time, and so far too young for the position of king, and Antigonus had placed himself beyond pardon by bringing in the Parthians. Of any other claimants to the Hasmonean throne Herod had the best claim by reason of his marriage.

One difficulty faced Herod the Romans had almost certainly never realized. Ever since Zerubbabel had disappeared from the scene, the leading figure in the Jewish commonwealth had been the high priest; in one sense the Hasmoneans had been high priests first and kings afterwards. It was impossible for Herod to be priest. With the Hasmoneans it was possible for the majority to overlook that they had no claim to the Davidic throne—apparently even the Qumran community did not object to them on this score—but once Herod was on the throne the hope of the Davidic Messiah came to full life once more.

The End of the Hasmoneans

As soon as Herod was firmly on the throne he executed Antigonus' leading supporters; in this his own desires and Roman expectations coincided. Since they were also the leaders of the Sadducean party, it meant that their political power received a blow from which it never recovered. He then took steps to neutralize any chance of popular support for the surviving Hasmoneans. He brought Hananel from Babylonia and made him high priest. We know nothing of his family, but in the setting it makes sense only if he belonged to a branch of the family from which Onias III, the last legitimate high priest, had come. He also encouraged Hyrcanus II to return from Parthia and treated him with the utmost honour.

His policy might well have met with popular acquiescence, if not approval, had Cleopatra and Alexandra not worked on Antony. The former hated Herod for having earlier insulted her and in addition wished to add Palestine to her Egyptian kingdom. The latter wanted the high-priesthood for her son Aristobulus. Under Antony's pressure Herod deposed Hananel—an evil omen for the future—and made Aristobulus high priest. A few months later he was drowned in a swimming pool at Jericho. There are no real grounds for thinking that it was other than an accident, but Herod's enemies then and later could not believe it was not deliberate murder.

The next six years were a time of strain and stress for Herod as the two royal ladies schemed ceaselessly against him, and Mariamne, whom he loved to distraction, grew ever colder. We do not know whether she was expressing her natural feelings, or whether she was being egged on by her mother.

The position changed completely when Octavian (Augustus) routed Antony decisively at Actium in 31 B.C. Herod waited on the victor and offered him his services and loyalty. In spite of his relationship to Antony he was accepted, and from then until his death in 4 B.C. his links with Augustus were close and harmonious. At home there was little border fighting or internal unrest. The Romans rewarded him by a steady increase in his territory. Just before Herod went to see Octavian he guarded his rear by putting Hyrcanus to death. He had always been an unwise man, torn between a desire for lack of responsibility and ease and ambitious dreams, so he may well have been listening to suggestions that his turn had come once again, now that Antony had fallen. On Herod's return his mother and sister so worked on him that he had Mariamne put to death and her mother the following year (28 B.C.).

From then on wide circles in Judea hated him bitterly as the ender of the house of Hasmon. This may not have troubled Herod, but he was given little peace by the intrigues of his sons against him and one another. The ordinary citizen was probably concerned far more by the continuing weight of taxation. This was probably less than in the last years of the Hasmoneans, for there were no wars to pay for, but Herod's grandiose building plans kept it heavy.

Herod as King

Herod saw himself in a double role. He was king of Judea, a term which in his lifetime came to include all Palestine on both sides of the Jordan, including the Hauran, except for most of the Decapolis, Ashkelon, and the coastal plain from Dor northwards. He was also King of the Jews and as such protector of the Jews in the Roman diaspora. Note that Matt. 2:1 carefully gives him neither title.

As King of the Jews he was able to gain the right for Jews outside Palestine to live according to the Mosaic law; after his death the Romans continued this policy towards Jews living in their empire. This was not a mere question of expediency, cf. Julius Caesar's grant of privileges in 47 B.C. In 15 B.C. Agrippa,

Augustus' son-in-law, came to Jerusalem and made a great sacrifice to the God of the Jews in the Temple. This shows that for the cultured Roman Judaism was seen as a respectable religion; this was one reason for the number of "God-fearers" we meet in Acts.

It is essential to realize that Herod was a religious Jew—we are not given to read his heart and know what he really thought about God. When he was besieging Jerusalem, when it was in the hands of Antigonus, he sent in sacrificial animals for the Temple sacrifices (*Ant*. XIV. xvi. 2). With all his honouring of Augustus he did not place his image on any coin he minted, noï was any public portrait of him allowed in Jerusalem. There does not seem to be any evidence that he took part in the worship of the pagan temples he had built. When he sent his sons to Rome, he had them educated with other Jewish boys there. Even Augustus' pun, quoted earlier, that he would prefer to be Herod's pig than his son, gains its point from the fact that he knew that the pig would be safe, because Herod would not eat pork.

As King of Judea he tried to strengthen, enrich and beautify his kingdom. Only a fraction of his building operations can be mentioned here. Masada is today the best known of his fortresses. He rebuilt Samaria (a Greek rather than a Samaritan city) and gave Palestine its first good port by building Caesarea on the Mediterranean coast. In Jerusalem he built himself a palace, of which the Citadel and "Tower of David" today are traces. His most famous project was the rebuilding of the Temple and its immediate surroundings. Both the great platform of the Haram es-Sherif and the West Wall are Herodian in origin. The work was begun in 19 B.C. and was not completed till A.D. 63, cf. Jn. 2 : 20, though the main work was finished before his death.

He tried to treat his Jewish, Samaritan and Gentile subjects equally. When he built Caesarea, he intended it to be half Jewish, half Gentile in population, and for the latter he built a temple to Augustus and Rome in it. He instituted the Actian Games to be held every four years at Jerusalem in honour of Augustus' victory at Actium and built for them a hippodrome within the city walls, a theatre some distance south of them and an amphitheatre a little further away.

It is not hard to understand his motives. He had no wish to Hellenize the Jews by force as Antiochus Epiphanes had tried so disastrously to do, but he wished to bring them sufficiently out of their isolation to create a unitary kingdom. A purely Jewish Palestine had become a fanatic's dream, and so the disparate elements had to be brought closer together. There was also a growing gap between the Palestinian Jew and the Jewish diaspora. This wish to make his kingdom part of the culture that surrounded it lay behind his generous gifts to famous cities, e.g. Athens, Antioch, Rhodes, and his becoming a major benefactor of the Olympic games.

Such a king had no respect for traditional interpretations of the Mosaic law. Apparently he was loyal enough to it not to have gladiatorial shows in which man fought man, but he pitted gladiators, and especially condemned criminals, against wild beasts, which the religious Jew considered a contradiction of man's worth as created in the image of God. Then, in his dealings with burglars and highwaymen, whom the troubled times had caused to proliferate, he sold those that could not make restitution to foreigners instead of Jews, thus involving them in lifelong slavery instead of only six years servitude. It is hard to know how much ill-will he caused by his treatment of the high-priesthood. His record was certainly better than that of his successors, Roman and Herodian.

Jewish Religious Parties Under Herod

When the Judean state emerged under Simon the Hasmonean, there were apparently few far-reaching religious divisions within it. The Hellenists had either been murdered during the long struggle for freedom or had been forced to flee the land. On the remainder of the population Ezra's reforms had worked as a unifying power. The differences that existed were mainly social and economic. Even though the leading priestly families had their traditions that were not necessarily shared by the mainly non-ecclesiastical Pharisees, it was for social and political reasons that John Hyrcanus turned to them, the Sadducees as they came to be called. As so often happens, religion was appealed to to justify political differences, but down to the time of the Roman take-over the conflict had been a mainly secular one. In fact, when we study the points at issue between Pharisees and Sadducees as recorded in the Talmud—they are few—it becomes very difficult to believe that their hostility was ever primarily religious.

Even with the Essenes of Qumran a genuine religious split was slow in developing. Undoubtedly the assumption of the high-priesthood by Simon the Hasmonean had deeply shocked their legitimist principles, a shock doubtless the greater because some of their leaders will have lost lucrative positions in the change, but they apparently remained within the official religious community until Alexander Jannai had shown himself completely unworthy of the respect of any truly religious man. It was then that the Teacher of Righteousness had shown them a theological justification for withdrawal from corporate society.

The Roman take-over greatly reduced the political importance of the two main parties. Herod's triumph and the massacre of Antigonus' supporters that accompanied it broke the political power of the Sadducees completely. They remained the dominant force in the Temple, and they were used by the Romans, when it suited them, but henceforth their real importance lay in their maintenance of ancient priestly traditions.

Religiously Herod was clearly neutral. He could have invited the high-priestly descendants of Onias IV to return from their temple in Leontopolis in Egypt, but that would have set up a possible rival to his power. We have seen that his first high priest, Hananel, will probably have been linked with the legitimate high-priestly line. After the premature death of Aristobulus III he was restored and probably died in office. He was followed by an obscure figure, Jesus son of Phiabi, who was deposed, so that Simon, son of Boethus, father of Herod's new wife, Mariamne II, might take his place. Twenty-four high priests were to follow during the existence of the Temple and of these only four families account for eighteen of them. Since, however, the earlier rabbinic writings clearly use Sadducees and Boethusians as synonyms, it is a reasonable supposition that these four families were linked by marriage at the very least; probably the connection was even closer. Boethus, or his son Simon, came from Egypt, which suggests that the family had been loyal to Onias IV and was probably linked to him by blood.

If this is so, it would show Herod favouring legitimacy, so long as it did not threaten his position. This in turn made it easier for the Essenes to return from Qumran. Their later withdrawal back to Qumran may be fairly confidently linked with the Roman assumption of direct rule over Judea in A.D. 6, which for them was a clear sign that they had entered the last days. This view of Herod's treatment of the high-priesthood is a contradiction of Josephus' statement, "Herod . . . made certain men to be (high priests) that were of no eminent families, but barely of them that were priests . . ." (*Ant.* XX. x. 1). Josephus found it hard to say anything good of Herod; in addition he was a great admirer of the Hasmoneans and proud to be a Pharisee, so we may doubt the objectivity of his opinions in such matters.

The Pharisees, who had been forced into politics largely by accident, had learnt a bitter lesson at the hands of Alexander Jannai and had been deeply shocked by the way Israel had been torn asunder under Hyrcanus and Aristobulus. Hence many of them saw in Herod the man who could give them peace and the elimination of their deadly enemies. While Herod was besieging Jerusalem, Shemayah and his pupil Hillel had advised the citizens to admit him, so later, when Hillel and Shammai refused to give an oath of loyalty to Rome, Herod relieved them and their disciples of the necessity (*Ant.* XV. x. 4).

This is not to suggest that the Pharisaic leaders approved of Herod. Far from it, but they regarded the rule of Rome as a righteous judgment from God and Herod's religious neutrality as their opportunity for turning the hearts of the people to God and His Law. It is no accident that later rabbis looked back to Hillel and Shammai as the real formulators of their distinctive system.

The Essenes too were released from any obligation to take the oath. This was partly because they considered that any such oath involved taking the name of God in vain (*War* II. viii. 6). More important, perhaps, to Herod was that they accepted the ruler, however good or bad, because he had been appointed by the will of God (*ibid. 7*, cf. Rom. 13 : 1, 2).

Josephus drew on a number of sources and he sometimes combined them clumsily. Hence, though he usually wrote eulogistically of the Pharisees, we find the unexpected condemnation in *Ant.* XVII. ii. 4, "For there was a certain sect . . . who valued themselves highly upon the exact skill they had in the law of their fathers . . . They are called the sect of the Pharisees, who were in a capacity of greatly opposing kings. A cunning sect they were and soon elevated to a pitch of open fighting, and doing mischief". He tells us too that when they refused to take the oath of allegiance they were fined, and when Herod found that they were prophesying the end of his rule, he executed their leaders.

Josephus was indubitably correct in calling them Pharisees, but in one vital point they had a different outlook from that of the disciples of Hillel and Shammai. Though they were devoted to the Law, they laid an equal or even greater stress on the kingship of God. We can probably hear their voice in the Psalms of Solomon, written shortly after the death of Pompey in 48 B.C.; they rejoice over God's judgment on the man who had brought shame on the name of God by subjecting Judea and entering the Temple. There is no evidence that they were prepared to take arms against Herod, for they were expecting supernatural deliverance through the Messiah, but they were certainly bitterly opposed to him.

It could well be that those who conspired against Herod, when he first built his theatre in Jerusalem (*Ant.* XV. viii. 1–4), belonged to this group. Almost certainly Judas and Matthias belonged to them. They were popular teachers who, when they thought Herod was on his death-bed, encouraged their pupils to tear down the golden eagle Herod had placed over the great gate of the Temple. Even though he was near his end, Herod rallied sufficiently to have the two teachers and those directly involved burnt alive and ordered others implicated to be executed (*War* I. xxxiii. 2, 3).

It was from these circles that the Zealots sprang. For them the kingship of God took precedence over the keeping of the Law, even though this was deeply honoured. In ch. 15 we saw that already during the reign of Hyrcanus II Herod, as his father's representative in Galilee, had trouble with Hezekiah, the leader of a band of "robbers", whom he summarily executed with his men. Josephus respected the Zealots' teaching deeply, though he detested many of their actions. Hence, when he wrote of their principles, he did not identify them by name but wrote of "the fourth sect of Jewish philosophy" (*Ant.* XVIII. i. 6). In attributing the origin of their views to Judas the Galilean he almost certainly meant Judas the son of Hezekiah. Shortly after Herod's death he was able to seize Sepphoris, the capital of Galilee, and claim the "royal dignity" (*Ant.* XVII. x. 5). Though he was not able to hold his position long, it shows how he had been able to build up a considerable following in spite of the activity of Herod's spies.

No sooner was Herod dead than the kingdom he had built up began to dissolve. This was helped by the poor quality of the men Rome sent out as its representatives, but had they been of the highest calibre they would have only delayed the final tragedy. Only a man of Herod's understanding, will-power and ruthlessness could have done what he was able to do. In God's purpose he gave Israel a breathing space in which they could draw the lesson from the failure of the outward keeping of the Law, of the possession of an Aaronic priesthood and Temple cultus and of kingship and national freedom. The opportunity was accepted by the few, and so the second Commonwealth was doomed to pass even as the first had, when Jerusalem fell to Nebuchadnezzar.

ADDITIONAL NOTE

The Religious Position at the Death of Herod

A summary of the religious groupings at the beginning of the first century A.D. may be useful.

The great difference between the religion of Palestinian Jewry (and indeed of the Eastern diaspora and probably a majority of Jews in the West) and early

Christianity, once it had become firmly based in the Greek cities of the Eastern Mediterranean, was that the former had very little philosophical speculation on the facts of its faith. It is going too far to say that Judaism had no theology, but it was mainly concerned with behaviour. What little speculation there was in smaller circles was more mystic than philosophic.

It is popular today to contrast Hellenistic Judaism with the Judaism of Palestine and the East. The latest work on the subject, *The Jewish People in the First Century*, edited by S. Safrai and M. Stern, shows in the chapters on *The Jewish Diaspora* and *Relations between the Diaspora and the Land of Israel* that there was far less of a cleavage than is often suggested. The actions of the Hellenists in the time of Antiochus Epiphanes, cf. ch. 12, brought such opprobrium on them, that even in Alexandria or Asia Minor strict adherence to at least the externals of the Mosaic Law was expected of those who wished to be known as Jews. Only then was it possible to play with Greek thought as well. For the mass of the Jews in the Western diaspora there will have been little obvious division, beyond language, between them and their fellow-countrymen in Palestine.

The Sadducees were probably almost entirely confined to Palestine. They belonged virtually entirely to the richer priestly families, who dominated the Temple worship, and the wealthy families with which they were linked by marriage. They were proud to be the inheritors of ancient traditions, mainly cultic but also legal, which were not infrequently in conflict with the opinions of those who stood in the inheritance of Ezra. Their power came from the unique position of the High Priest, and once this was undermined, they faced, like all conservative authoritarian autocrats, inevitable defeat. Their basic authority was the Pentateuch as expounded by their traditions. If they publicly rejected the possibility of the resurrection of the dead, cf. Mk. 12:18, it was probably less a conviction and more an affirmation based on the apparent impossibility of proving it from the Pentateuch alone (but cf. Mk. 12:26, 27). They regarded the prophetic books as having devotional but not authoritative value. Their ill-fame among the masses came especially from the rigour with which they applied their interpretation of the Law, which made no allowances for the poor and needy.

Opposed to them were those who considered that the Torah interpreted from within itself and by the aid of the prophetic books could be made to cover the whole of life. They considered that such interpretations must override Sadducean traditions, however venerable they might be—in fact, wherever details have come down to us, the differences between the two sides seem to be unimportant. The main difference was that the Sadducees presented themselves as the authoritarian enforcers of the Law, while their opponents considered that the Law was open for the study and understanding of all who had the preparation and leisure. Apart, however, from a general uniformity in the manner of life, we cannot speak of a united opposition.

The Essenes of Qumran were concerned above all with the legitimacy of the High Priest, so it is not surprising that the backbone of their movement seems to have consisted of priests and Levites. So far as the practical application of the Torah was concerned they were rigorists. Their special views were derived from the interpretation of the Prophets (not the Torah) given by the Teacher of Righteousness, aided by their conviction that they were living in the last days.

The name Pharisees almost certainly means "separated ones" and at the first ·was probably a name given them by their enemies. This separation, in some ways as real as that of the Essenes, was due to their insistence on outward purity and ritually pure food, especial insistence being laid on proof that the tithing process had been carried out. There were probably from the first varying groups, but by the beginning of the Christian era these had crystallized round the two great teachers Shammai and Hillel. Shammai was wealthy and of good family and he advocated rigour in the interpretation and enforcement of the Torah. Hillel, a poor man, of whose Babylonian background we know virtually nothing, took the part of the poor, and with them in mind made his interpretation of Torah as merciful as possible. It is easy to understand why, apart from a strictly limited number of rulings, the views of Hillel and his disciples carried the day. Had they not, Pharisaism would never have become the dominant power in Jewry after the collapse of the state, nor would the masses gradually have accepted "the yoke of the Law", cf. Acts 15 : 10.

In Galilee with its mainly proletarian society Pharisaism may have been admired by many, but grinding poverty made the transformation of society a more attractive vision. So it was taken for granted by the religious leaders in Jerusalem that the observance of the laws of ritual purity could not be assumed for Galilee. The Zealots will have understood "the kingdom of heaven" in this way, and they will have read an advocacy of violent action into Matt. 11 : 12. It is clear, however, that they tried to keep the demands of the Torah, where they considered it practically possible. G. Vermes in ch. 3 of *Jesus the Jew* argues for a considerable element of the charismatic in Galilee at the time.

A considerable element of the population both among the poor and the richer landowners were more concerned with living than religion, though they will have given their conformity to accepted standards, but their determined opposition to Pharisaic demands during the earlier portion of the second century A.D. shows how little they really shared their ideals. This opposition must not be interpreted in all cases as a sign of materialism.

18

ICHABOD!

Josephus reports (*Ant*. XVII. vi. 5, *War* I. xxxiii. 33) that when Herod realized that he was on his death-bed, he had all the Jewish leaders gathered together in the hippodrome at Jericho under strict military guard and ordered that, as he breathed his last, they should to the last man be put to the sword. He said grimly that he would be accompanied to the grave by universal mourning, because of him, if not for him. Through the efforts of Salome, his sister, who had stood by him through thick and thin, and Archelaus, his chief heir, the order was countermanded.

If the story is true, as it may well be, it can be explained by Herod's madness due to the pain of his disease-racked body. It could, however, be that he had realized the shortcomings of Archelaus, who had become his successor designate only because so many of his other sons had over the years been bloodily eliminated, and because he knew that only by terror would his son be able to maintain his position. In his will he had left him only Judea with Idumea and Samaria, while he had divided the rest of his kingdom between Philip and Antipater. His will was upheld by Augustus, who, however, refused Archelaus the title of king. He had to be satisfied with that of ethnarch until he had demonstrated his ability to rule. His brothers had to accept that of tetrarch.

Had Herod died only a little later, it is possible that Archelaus might have weathered the storm; it was his dying shortly before the Passover pilgrims were due in Jerusalem that was fatal for his son. At the funeral feast he was able to win the approval of the men of Jerusalem. With the Passover, however, the Zealots came from Galilee, and they were harder to satisfy. They demanded harsh measures against Herod's advisers and the deposition of the High Priest. Archelaus felt, probably wisely, that he had to refuse. In the ensuing riot some three thousand were killed in the Temple. The people were so stunned by this that Archelaus had time to go to Rome to obtain the emperor's ratification of his father's will. Unfortunately the opposition caused by the ambitions of Herod Antipas so delayed Augustus' decision that troubles broke out at home.

These were caused in the first place by the greed of Sabinus and Varus, the procurator and legate of Syria respectively. At Pentecost fighting broke out in Jerusalem, and part of the cloisters round the Court of the Gentiles was burnt down. The Romans took the opportunity to seize the Temple treasure. This was followed by troubles throughout Palestine. Some of the risings were anti-Roman; others, like the seizure of Sepphoris by Judas the Zealot (cf. p. 117), were mainly religious in nature. The trouble is that we owe our information to Josephus (*Ant*. XVII. x. 4–8), who cannot be relied on to give us the true motivation. Varus was able to impose a semblance of peace but gave a grim warning of the power of Rome by crucifying two thousand of the insurgents.

The arguments going on in Rome were further complicated by a delegation from Jerusalem, which had come by permission of Varus. Josephus tells us that it was joined by eight thousand of the Jews living in Rome (*Ant.* XVII. xi. 1). Their request was that Palestine should become part of the Roman province of Syria, but that they should be allowed to live under their own (religious) laws. The underlying concept was clearly that they should be allowed to revert to the position they had had for so long under the Persians and the Ptolemies, i.e. complete religious and cultural autonomy under the high-priestly supervision, cf. p. 95. Some, e.g. Oesterley, see the less militant Pharisees behind the delegation, others, e.g. Klausner, the leaders of popular opinion. There can be little doubt, however, that Zeitlin is correct in recognizing it as Sadducean, with Joazar son of Boethus, the High Priest, as its main inspirer. After the recent troubles Pharisees would not have welcomed Sadducean rule. Zeitlin explains the support given by the Jews of Rome reasonably enough by their desire not to be suspected of disloyalty to Rome. If the foreign policy of Palestine were completely in Roman hands, they could not be accused of secretly favouring the Parthians.*

Direct Roman Rule

Ten years later this request was granted, when, after a joint complaint by Jews and Samaritans about his rule, Archelaus was deposed by the emperor and sent into exile. Judea and Samaria were constituted a special district under a procurator, who was under the general supervision of the legate of Syria.

It soon became apparent how seriously those behind the delegation had misjudged the situation. In the immediate post-exilic situation under the Persians, once the Davidic house had retreated into obscurity, the high priests were the only legitimate authority within Jewry. The Qumranic schism shows how greatly their position was weakened once the office had been taken over by the Hasmoneans. It was reduced even further, when Herod, Archelaus and then the Romans deposed and appointed high priests to suit their pockets and their policies. While the Romans had no interest in interfering with Jewish religious law, they saw to it that the religious leaders offered no opposition to their demands.

Josephus, trying to put the position in a more favourable light for his Gentile readers, said that the government was an aristocracy ruled by the high priests (*Ant.* XX. x. 5). Zeitlin's commentary on it is quite fair, "The government of Judaea was a combination of timocracy—the love for the ruler—and nomocracy—the rule of law. The high priests who headed the community were lovers of Rome, while the daily life of the people was ruled by the *Bet Din haGadol* and its religious enactments."† In fact, however, if there were a clash of interests, the Roman will would normally triumph.

The subservience of the Sadducean priesthood to the Romans made it ever

* *The Rise and Fall of the Judaean State*, Vol. II, pp. 127f.

† *op. cit.*, p. 139.

more difficult for it to resist the Pharisaic pressure for innovations in the interpretation of the Law. The price the Pharisees had to pay for having their
way was some measure of political cooperation with the Sadducean rulers. It
was this that made the scandal of the condemnation of Jesus of Nazareth possible. It also alienated the bulk of the people, especially in Galilee, who grew
increasingly sympathetic towards the Zealots, who combined observance of
the Mosaic Law with a rejection of any and every authority recognized by and
recognizing the Romans.

There was an almost immediate indication of what Roman rule involved in
practice. The deposition of Archelaus coincided with a census taken by Quirinius in the province of Syria. The Roman attitude was clearly and brutally
shown by the inclusion of the semi-independent territories of Philip and Herod
Antipas with Judea, now under direct Roman rule. The census raised threefold
opposition. It demonstrated firstly in the most obvious way that the Jews were
under heathen rule. Then it was clearly realized that the main purpose behind
it was taxation, which is never welcomed. Finally it offended deep-rooted
Jewish religious susceptibilities. In Judea the opposition was quieted by the
high priest (*Ant.* XVIII.i.1), though Quirinius, in typical Roman fashion,
showed his "gratitude" by deposing him. In Galilee Judas, who had seized Sepphoris after Herod's death, but had managed to escape when the Romans
turned against him, raised a major revolt, which ended in his death (Acts
5:37). This was not the census of Luke 2:1, 2, about which nothing definitive
can be said at present in spite of much scholarly investigation and argument.*

In the sixty years between the deposition of Archelaus and the outbreak of
the great revolt against Rome (A.D. 66) there was only one short period of
nominally Jewish rule in Jerusalem. Herod Agrippa I (Acts 12:1–23) was a
grandson of Herod the Great and brother of Herodias (Mk. 6:17), who had
married first her uncle Herod Philip (not Philip the Tetrarch, but a brother of
the same name) and then his half brother Herod Antipas. After a series of
almost incredible adventures Agrippa was made king of the tetrarchies that had
been ruled by Philip and Lysanias by the emperor Caligula (A.D. 37). Two
years later, when Herod Antipas was deposed and exiled, his tetrarchy was
added to Antipas' kingdom. Only four years after he had become king, Gaius
added Judea and Samaria, so Agrippa found himself king of virtually the whole
area ruled by his grandfather. He was able to win the confidence of the Pharisees, whom he favoured at the expense of the Sadducean high priests, who
naturally resented their loss of influence. In all probability the Pharisees shut
their eyes to the fact that among Gentiles Agrippa behaved virtually as a Gentile. His sudden and premature death in A.D. 44 destroyed the last hope of an
even nominally independent Judea, for his son, Herod Agrippa II (Acts 25:13),
was too young to follow him, and the territory he was later to rule was mainly
to the north of Palestine. Had the revolt been delayed, it is just possible that he
would have been given his father's kingdom. As it was, the whole of Palestine

---

* The often-heard suggestion that Luke was here making a historical confusion overlooks the fact that the
strongly Aramaic nature of his first two chapters suggests a story told by eye-witnesses, probably including
Mary.

came under direct Roman rule in A.D. 44.

History records the names of fourteen Roman procurators of Judea, seven before Herod Agrippa I, who governed only the centre and south, and seven after him, who governed the whole country. Some of them are known to us by name only—it is striking that the first contemporary mention of Pontius Pilate, outside the New Testament, Philo and Josephus, was found only in 1961 during excavations at Caesarea*—and of none is anything particularly good recorded, and of many much that is positively evil. This is not hard to understand, for Judea was never more than a third-rate district, and the procurators were normally more interested in enriching themselves that in anything else, though normally they tried to keep the peace so as to avoid being recalled by the emperor. The fact is that Rome did not have any large number of really able provincial administrators, and the emperors did not see why they should be wasted on Judea.

The bringing of Galilee under direct Roman rule angered the Zealots, who were strongest there, and increased their general influence. As a result each of the seven procurators during the twenty years before the outbreak of the great revolt had Zealot uprisings to quell. In one of them Alexander, an apostate Jew from a leading Jewish family in Alexandria, put two of the sons of Judas to death (46–48).

The last procurator, Florus, was not merely brutal and venal but also incompetent. We have grounds for thinking that he wanted to goad the Jews to revolt, so that his pickings might be the greater. In August 66 sacrifices for the Roman emperor were discontinued. Florus' mishandling of the situation made any peaceful solution impossible. At first it seemed that the Romans might be thrown out of the land, at least for the time being, but the arrival of Vespasian in the spring of 67 changed the picture almost immediately. Before the end of the year Galilee was in his hands, and by the spring of 68 the western parts of Judea, Idumea and Perea had fallen to him.

Jerusalem was not immediately attacked. This was partly due to Nero's suicide in June; Vespasian wanted to see what would follow, before he involved his forces in the siege of Jerusalem. In addition he knew that events were fighting for him there. In the city and even in the Temple moderates fought nationalists, while the Zealots, divided into three groups, fought one another and all others.

By June 69 the only area left to the insurgents was Jerusalem and the three almost impregnable Herodian fortresses, Herodion, Masada and Machaerus. Vespasian left for Rome to be hailed as emperor and left his son Titus in charge. Shortly before Passover in April 70 Titus appeared before Jerusalem and invested it. The day that many of the fanatics believed could not come had come. The final agony was not to last long, cf. Matt. 24:22. On Aug. 29, the anniversary of the destruction of the Temple by the Babylonians (*Tisha b'Av*), the sanctuary was set on fire and destroyed. Within a month the whole city was

---

* A reproduction of the inscription may be found on Plate XI in F. F. Bruce, *Israel and the Nations*; for a general discussion of the evidence see Schürer, *The History of the Jewish People in the Age of Jesus Christ* Vol. I, pp. 383–387, M. Grant, *The Jews in the Roman World*, pp. 99–102.

in Roman hands. With the capture of Masada in April 73 this chapter of Israel's history was finally closed.

Josephus, who was in a good position to know, estimated that a million one hundred thousand Jews had been killed and 97,000 taken away as slaves. Though we have consistently hesitated to accept his figures as exaggerations, here we may rather suspect an underestimate. We must not forget the many older people who died of famine or were put to death by their captors as being useless as slaves. Equally the estimate is not likely to include all who perished in the bitter feuds in Jerusalem itself. In any case two generations had to pass before Palestinian Jewry felt able to challenge the might of Rome for the second and final time.

The crushing of the nationalists, the virtual annihilation of the Zealots and the assassination of the Sadducean leaders meant that the religious leadership now fell almost uncontested into the hands of the more moderate Pharisees. This was further helped by the bloody suppression of Jewish revolts in Egypt and Cyrene, Cyprus and Mesopotamia (115–117) and was sealed by the disaster of Bar Kochba's revolt (132–5). From then on Jewish nationalism became little more than an eschatological hope until little more than a century ago.

BIBLIOGRAPHY
GENEALOGICAL TABLES
AND INDEXES

BIBLIOGRAPHY

W. F. Albright, *Archaeology of Palestine* (revised edition)
S. Benko & J. J. O'Rourke, *Early Church History*
A. Bentzen, *Introduction to the Old Testament*
J. Bright, *A History of Israel*[2]
R. Brinker, *The Influence of Sanctuaries in Early Judaism*
L. E. Browne, *Early Judaism*
F. F. Bruce, *Israel and the Nations*
  Second Thoughts on the Dead Sea Scrolls[3]
E. W. Bullinger, *The Companion Bible*
L. Finkelstein, *The Pharisees*[3]
R. L. Fox, *Alexander the Great*
D. N. Freedman & Greenfield, *New Directions in Biblical Archaeology*
M. Grant, *The Jews in the Roman World*
P. E. Kahle, *The Cairo Geniza*
J. Klausner, *Jesus of Nazareth*
C. G. Montefiore & H. Loewe, *A Rabbinic Anthology*
M. Noth, *The History of Israel*[2]
W. O. E. Oesterley & T. H. Robinson, *A History of Israel*, Vol. II
R. H. Pfeiffer, *History of New Testament Times*
W. M. Ramsay, *Cities of Saint Paul*
B. J. Roberts, *The Old Testament Text and Versions*
H. H. Rowley, *The Servant of the Lord*
W. Rudolph, *Esra und Nehemia*
J. C. Rylaarsdam, *Revelation in Jewish Wisdom Literature*
S. Safrai & M. Stern, *The Jewish People in the First Century*, Vol. I
E. Schürer, *The History of the Jewish People in the Age of Jesus Christ*[4], Vol. I
  (revised)

N. H. Snaith, *Studies in the Psalter*
J. C. Stobart, *The Glory that was Greece*
D. Winton Thomas, *Documents from Old Testament Times*
G. Vermes, *Jesus the Jew*
R. J. Z. Werblowsky & G. Wigoder, *The Encyclopedia of the Jewish Religion*
J. Stafford Wright, *The Date of Ezra's Coming to Jerusalem*
S. Zeitlin, *The Rise and Fall of the Judaean State*, Vols. I & II

GENEALOGICAL TABLES

THE HASMONAEAN FAMILY

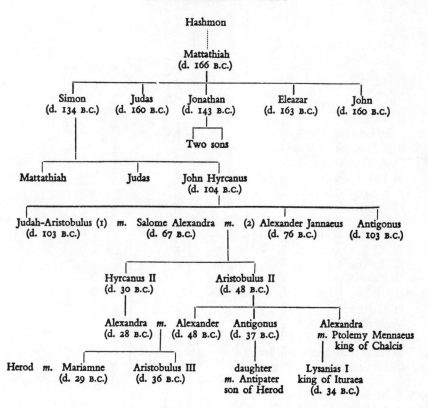

Hashmon

Mattathiah
(d. 166 B.C.)

Simon (d. 134 B.C.)   Judas (d. 160 B.C.)   Jonathan (d. 143 B.C.)   Eleazar (d. 163 B.C.)   John (d. 160 B.C.)

Two sons

Mattathiah   Judas   John Hyrcanus (d. 104 B.C.)

Judah-Aristobulus (1) (d. 103 B.C.)   *m.*   Salome Alexandra (d. 67 B.C.)   *m.*   (2) Alexander Jannaeus (d. 76 B.C.)   Antigonus (d. 103 B.C.)

Hyrcanus II (d. 30 B.C.)   Aristobulus II (d. 48 B.C.)

Alexandra (d. 28 B.C.)   *m.*   Alexander (d. 48 B.C.)   Antigonus (d. 37 B.C.)   Alexandra *m.* Ptolemy Mennaeus king of Chalcis

Herod   *m.*   Mariamne (d. 29 B.C.)   Aristobulus III (d. 36 B.C.)   daughter *m.* Antipater son of Herod   Lysanias I king of Ituraea (d. 34 B.C.)

HEROD'S ANCESTRY AND KIN

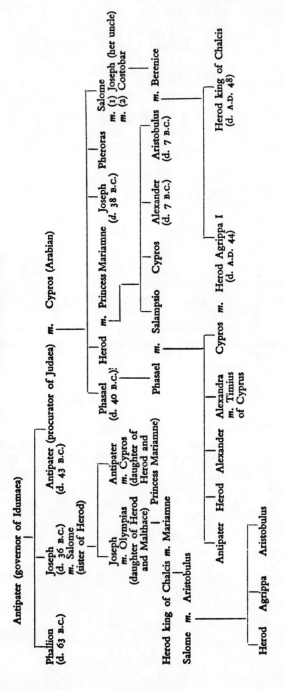

DESCENDANTS OF HEROD AND PRINCESS MARIAMNE

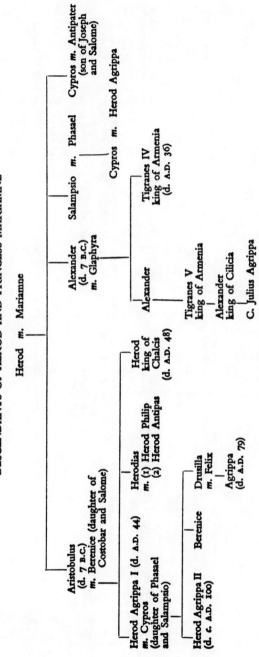

SOME DESCENDANTS OF HEROD BY OTHER WIVES

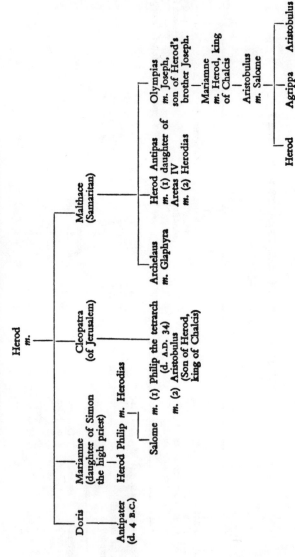

GENERAL INDEX

INDEX OF REFERENCES

BIBLICAL

APOCRYPHA AND PSEUDEPIGRAPHA

RABBINIC SOURCES

JOSEPHUS